The *joy* of LIVING

Postponing the Afterlife

Barry Eaton
and Anne Morjanoff

ROCKPOOL
PUBLISHING

A Rockpool book
PO Box 252
Summer Hill
NSW 2130
Australia
www.rockpoolpublishing.com.au
http://www.facebook.com/RockpoolPublishing

First published in 2017
Copyright text © Barry Eaton and Anne Morjanoff 2017
This edition published in 2017

National Library of Australia Cataloguing-in-Publication entry

Eaton, Barry, author.

The joy of living : postponing the afterlife / Barry Eaton,
Anne Morjanoff.

ISBN: 9781925429480 (paperback)

Eaton, Barry.
Cancer–Patients–Australia–Anecdotes.
Throat–Diseases–Diagnosis.
Throat–Diseases–Alternative treatment.
Life change events.
Holistic medicine.
Mind and body.

Other Creators/Contributors:
Morjanoff, Anne, author.

Cover design by Farrah Careem
Cover image by Pexels and Shutterstock
Typeset by Typeskill
Printed and bound in China

10 9 8 7 6 5 4 3 2 1

Contents

Introduction

Cancer. Often referred to as The Big C.

The word carries a unique energy as well as the implication that is terrifying. As the number of lives affected by cancer increases around the globe every year, it is hard to find someone in our circle of family, friends and colleagues whose lives have not been touched in some way.

Statistics released by the World Health Organisation (WHO) showed that cancer is a leading cause of death worldwide, accounting for 8.2 million deaths in 2012. The same report revealed that some 14 million people are diagnosed with cancer every year, and that number is expected to rise by about 70 per cent over the next two decades. The statistic that stood out for me was that more people die from cancer-related causes than are healed.

Fortunately, many lives affected by cancer *are* being saved as medical science makes great advances in this field. However, mainstream medicine tends to rely mainly on such practices as surgery, chemotherapy and radiotherapy. The WHO is urging the medical profession to accept that solutions for *preventing* cancer must be found as a matter of urgency.

The WHO report (at http://www.who.int/mediacentre/factsheets/fs297/en/) states that about 30 per cent of cancer deaths are due to five leading behavioural and dietary risks: high body mass index, low fruit and vegetable intake, lack of physical activity, tobacco use and alcohol use.

Tobacco is the most important risk factor for cancer, causing over 20 per cent of cancer deaths overall and about 70 per cent of deaths from lung cancer. Other leading causes of deaths are liver, stomach, colorectal, breast and oesophageal cancers, accounting for another third of all cancer deaths. It is not surprising that WHO is asking for urgent preventive solutions.

Many of us don't realise it but, as the WHO report states, 'cancer arises from one single cell. The transformation from a normal cell into a tumour cell is a multistage process, typically a progression from a pre-cancerous lesion to malignant tumours.'

One cell, one rogue cell, can change your life forever. It seems hard to believe.

There are many claims of alternative treatments for cancer. They are usually dismissed out of hand by most mainstream medical authorities, who traditionally advocate scientific and pharmaceutical treatments. This is not surprising as the cancer industry in the United States alone is estimated to be worth over $200 billion a year. Many sceptics believe that those in positions of power are not interested in delivering a cure as it would be financially disastrous for the cancer industry. Unfortunately it is hard to know just how effective alternative treatments are, as this information is not readily available, apart from isolated claims and some anecdotal reports on the internet. The medical establishment tends to dismiss complementary or alternative treatments out of hand, unless combined with conventional practices.

However, detailed information about the long-term effects of mainstream treatments is also very hazy. A patient is regarded as being in remission if there is no trace of cancer after a period of five years following treatment. If the cancer returns after that, it is apparently treated as a whole new ball game, which sounds very convenient.

My purpose in writing this book is to help inspire people facing the ordeal of cancer to realise that being diagnosed with this disease is not necessarily the beginning of the end. This is *my* story of how I came to terms with the Big C and the holistic way I prepared and coped with something that suddenly turned my life upside down. Of course everyone's experience of cancer is unique — no two cases are exactly the same.

The *Oxford Dictionary* defines cancer as 'from (the) Latin, "crab or creeping ulcer", translating Greek *karkinos*, said to have been applied to such tumours because the swollen veins around them resembled the limbs of a crab.' If my story helps just one person cope emotionally with this pervasive form of disease, then writing this book will have been worthwhile.

Looking back on the more than seventy years of my life, I have come to the firm conclusion that everything happens for a reason. We may not consciously choose to create problems, but I believe that we subconsciously create, attract or accept *everything* in our daily lives. Understanding and dealing with these events — good, bad and indifferent — and the wide range of people we encounter along the way, is an integral part of why we are here in the first place. Life is about having a multitude of positive and challenging human experiences and how we react to them physically, emotionally and spiritually. I have found that accepting responsibility for my thoughts, beliefs and actions is the most positive starting point in coping with life's ups and downs.

Over the years I have come to accept that it is all too easy to just go to a doctor and rely on a pharmaceutical prescription to solve my problems. The range of drugs, particularly for mental and emotional conditions, that some people end up swallowing daily is frightening. The side effects can be horrendous. Years ago I made a conscious decision to explore as many options as possible and not just rely on the pharmaceutical industry — or Big Pharma as it has become known — for a convenient answer to health problems. This has led me to explore the world of holistic or complementary medicine and I have found many solutions that have worked for me. Now I only take drugs, including painkillers, when it is absolutely imperative.

So when I was diagnosed with a cancerous growth in the throat in early 2013, I was faced with a dilemma. I thought, as a researcher and believer in natural and holistic healing modalities, do I dig my heels in against traditional medical practices as a matter of principle?

Inevitably, the initial response to being diagnosed with any form of cancer is to retreat into fear mode. I was no different to anyone else in this regard. However, several years ago I discovered a useful acronym for FEAR — False Evidence Appearing Real —and digging deep I have usually been able to work with this demon whenever it crops up. The vast majority of my past worries were false alarms, which soon dissipated when facts emerged or conditions changed. Indeed, for most of us, it's often difficult to remember what we were worried about even a few months later, as life moves on so fast. One set of worries usually dissolves into the next.

Having thoroughly researched the whole area of death in the course of writing two books on the afterlife, I felt no immediate fear of this when medical scans confirmed the existence of my cancer. But I did have to cope with other fears about the treatment process I was required to undergo in order to at least postpone my return to the afterlife. The way I was able to conquer these fears and emerge relatively unscathed from my intense treatments is the important part of my story. It was a journey in which I needed to be willing and able to accept the role that I had to play in the treatment and healing processes.

For many years, whenever the subject of cancer came up I had firmly stated that I would never undergo chemotherapy whatever the circumstances. So as far as I was concerned chemotherapy was off the table from day one. However surgery was the first hurdle I had to face, and with a 2.5 centimetre growth in the base of my throat that felt like it was swelling daily, this decision did not require a lot of deliberation. At the time I thought to myself, *if the damned thing keeps getting bigger I'll end up choking to death.*

But I had no idea what would happen after the initial surgery, as my mind just kept spinning and rejecting any long-term planning. Because I have a media background and am used to delving deep into a subject, I decided to do my own research before making any final decision. My first port of call was Cancer Council NSW, where the staff were most understanding and helpful. Then I researched all the potential alternative and complementary medicine practices I could find that related to my condition. My final and most important move was to do my inner exploration, as I rely very much on my intuition and inner wisdom in my daily life.

After a great deal of soul-searching and spiritual guidance, I eventually clambered down off my high perch and decided the best and most positive way forward was to combine my alternative and spiritual beliefs and practices with mainstream medicine. In recent years I had come to accept that creating balance in all things is more often than not a key factor in helping cope with the vicissitudes of life. When I told my family of my decision, they admitted that they were relieved and very surprised, having believed that I would stubbornly refuse the conservative advice of my doctors. I didn't realise how much of a medical rebel they regarded me.

One very important influence in my battle with cancer has been the role that family and friends played. The love and support I received during these often long and exhausting months played a vital part in being able to handle the emotional and physical roller coaster I found myself riding.

My partner Anne has been an integral part of the successful outcome and her personal story forms the second part of this book. It tells the other side of the whole journey: that of the carer. When I read her reflections I realised how I got so caught up in my own troubles that Anne's support was not fully appreciated at the time. My world closed in around me and her memories and reactions filled in the missing parts of the story that I was often unable to even recall, let alone write about. It is only now, three years after my treatment finished, that I can fully appreciate and understand the burden that supporting me had dumped on her shoulders. At the time I had no idea what she was going through, a message that I would like other cancer patients to take into consideration.

Anne's story has made me realise with the benefit of twenty/twenty hindsight that, yes, it's a tough time going through the cancer experience, but I was not the only one who was suffering.

My son Matt has been a pillar of strength too and he has written of the way the events unfolded from his perspective. And in the early stages my daughter Rebecca reminded me of a basic practice that also helped me enormously through the long medical process.

Looking back on the whole sequence of events, I now realise more than ever the importance of having a positive mindset. When I told Bec about my intention of writing this book, she enthusiastically encouraged me and reminded me that she had based her psychology PhD thesis on the broaden-and-build theory of positive emotion developed by the American psychologist Barbara Frederickson.

According to Wikipedia, Professor Frederickson's theory is based on the idea 'that emotions prepare the body both physically and psychologically to act in particular ways. For example, anger creates the urge to attack, fear causes an urge to escape and disgust leads to the urge to expel.' On the other hand, the theory implies that 'positive emotions have inherent value to human growth and development and cultivation of these emotions will help people lead fuller lives.' Barbara Fredrickson expanded her theory in a paper she wrote with Thomas Joiner entitled 'Positive Emotions Trigger Upward Spirals toward Emotional Well-Being'.

> The broaden-and-build theory of positive emotions predicts that positive emotions broaden the scopes of attention and cognition, and, by consequence, initiate upward spirals toward increasing emotional well-being.
>
> … If positive emotions broaden attention and cognition, enabling flexible and creative thinking, they should also facilitate coping with stress and adversity …
>
> … One way people experience positive emotions in the face of adversity is by finding positive meaning in ordinary events and within the adversity itself.

As I started my daunting journey, I was determined that my next book would not be written *from* the afterlife, the subject of my previous books.

PART I

Barry's Story

1

The Wait is Over

In the hospital waiting room, heart pounding and mind whirring, surrounded by a sea of apprehensive-looking fellow patients, I settled in to wait for my name to be called. Outside the sun was shining on a warm winter's afternoon, but I was anticipating a fairly long delay before I could break out of my surroundings and enjoy the unseasonal weather.

It has always intrigued me why we have to spend so much time in doctors' waiting rooms before appointments. It is a universal condition that I have come to expect. Maybe doctors get too involved with their patients to worry about time management. Even so, I always make sure I am on time, just in case the doctor is too.

To my surprise this was one of those occasions. I was jerked back to reality, abandoning the whirling dervishes of my thoughts, when I heard my name called. I looked up to see the tall, white-clad figure of a woman in her early thirties, holding a file in her right hand, which I presumed to be mine.

I followed her into her office thinking, *okay Barry, this is it*, as I held my breath waiting for the verdict. The doctor introduced herself as my oncologist's registrar, explaining that he was away that day. The look of concern must have been written all over my face as she opened my file and removed a sheet of paper.

'You can relax. Your latest scans are clear — they show that there is no further evidence of cancer in the treated area.'

These were the words I had waited to hear from the oncologist in Royal Brisbane and Women's Hospital for over six months. Six anxious, exhausting months, which at times seemed as if they would never end and which included three unexpected major surgical operations and seven weeks of intensive radiotherapy treatments.

In the days leading up to what I prayed was to be my final medical appointment, my nerves were still jangling, no matter how hard I tried to calm them. Even though intuitively I felt that the treatments were successful, there was this small nagging voice that popped into my head from time to time, whispering, *yes, but what if …?*

My son Matt and I had written two screenplays together and our director Michael Carson had always encouraged us to explore the what-if scenario when we were looking for potential plot developments. This phrase has now ingrained itself as a subconscious reaction whenever life takes a new twist. Actually, I come out with it all too often. My partner Anne often scolds me with, 'I don't want to go into any what ifs.'

When I heard those magic words that day, the relief swept over me like a cooling sea breeze on a hot summer's day as my stressful what ifs dissipated.

Twenty-four hours earlier I was lying on a hard bed, inside what the nuclear medicine staff at the hospital refer to as the 'doughnut', having a positron emission tomography (PET) scan. This is an imaging test that uses a small amount of radioactive material, called a tracer, which is given intravenously and travels through your blood, collecting in organs and tissues. This helps the radiologist see certain areas of concern more clearly. It was the ultimate check that would reveal whether the radiotherapy treatments I had undergone were successful in eradicating the cancer cells in my throat.

Stretched out on my back inside the tubular machine as the tray I was lying on slid in and out of the doughnut so multiple images of the affected are could be taken, my mind unconsciously slipped back to when it all began. The PET scan only took about twenty-five minutes, but in that time I was able to relive many of my experiences over those stressful months that had changed my life.

2

A Strange Beginning

It all started in January 2013. I had flown south to my home city of Sydney to attend the funeral of my cousin Russell, who had passed away after his own intense struggle with cancer.

It was a blisteringly hot summer day. Sitting with Anne in the cool interior of a country town cathedral for his funeral ceremony gave me pause to think about how life can change so suddenly. One day Russell was enjoying his quiet family life and the next the dreaded cancer began to take it all away. Waiting for the service to begin, my mind drifted. I wondered how my own life would end. I am not religious but, considering where we were sitting and for what, I sent a silent prayer of thanks to the universe for the generally good health I had enjoyed for most of my life.

Sure, like most people, I looked back on bouts of illness. In my case migraine headaches (relieved by hypnotherapy), lumbar problems in my lower back (eased by osteopaths) and recently diagnosed atrial fibrillation, or arrhythmia of the heart. None of them was life threatening. So I just took them in my stride and moved on with life. I felt very fortunate as we sat in the church trying to stay cool. Russell was a very conservative man, so to add to the stifling conditions I was clad in the obligatory jacket and tie, an attire I do my utmost to avoid at this stage of life.

Funerals and weddings are often the only time we catch up with many members of our family in these busy times, and any fleeting thoughts of my own demise soon disappeared as the service was followed by a happy celebration of Russell's life in the adjacent church hall. My family has always enjoyed a get-together with plenty of food and drink, and we were all determined to celebrate Russell's life. So, despite the intense heat, the afternoon was a happy time, tinged with sadness, but still lots of laughter was heard as the wake gathered steam. A lovely send-off, I mused, quite sure that Russell's spirit was floating about enjoying the occasion too. Russ, with his Welsh heritage, always enjoyed a party.

I reminded Anne that when it is my time I don't want a bunch of long-faced mourners at my funeral, just a group of good friends and relatives enjoying a fun time and swapping apocryphal stories of what a great person I was.

I woke up at Anne's place in Sydney a few days after the funeral and felt as if something had stuck in my throat. No matter what I did, it would not clear. Copious glasses of water and the odd glass of red wine had no impact, and my mother's old remedy of swallowing dry bread failed miserably (I did remember later that she said it mainly worked with fish bones stuck in the throat). So I tried to shrug off this annoying sensation and made strange guttural-type sounds trying to clear the blockage, which I laughingly referred to as like a cat trying to cough up a fur ball.

Returning to my home in northern New South Wales, the lump was getting more uncomfortable by the day. I tried coughing, tried to peer down my throat in the mirror and even tried sticking my fingers down my throat hoping that might clear the blockage. Nothing worked. *If it gets any bigger,* I thought, *I will choke to death.*

I finally relented and went to my local doctor. The look on his face made me realise it might be serious. He immediately sent me off to consult with Dr Tim, an ear, nose and throat (ENT) specialist. Thinking he would probably stick a pronged instrument down my throat and instantly remove some strange object that was stuck there, I recoiled a little when he poked a long cord down into my throat via the nasal passage. It was one of the most uncomfortable experiences I can remember as this cord snaked its way down my throat scraping on the sides and making me gag. The cord had a camera on the end of it and to my horror Dr Tim showed me a screen image of what he identified as a tumour at the base of my tongue, in an area he referred to as the lingual tonsil.

He told me that the tumour was most likely cancerous and would have to be surgically removed. A scan a few days later confirmed his diagnosis and he rang me with the bad news, immediately booking me into hospital for surgery a few days after that. It was only then that the seriousness of the situation dawned on me.

I don't remember a lot about the days leading up to the surgery, but I do remember feeling confident that once the tumour had been removed I would just get on with my life pretty much as before. Lying on the table just before I went into the operating theatre, I was joking with Dr Tim and the anaesthetist, whose nickname I discovered was Chook. I tend to become a bit flippant when I am nervous, but the banter we had helped settle my nerves as Chook put me to sleep. I counted one ... two ... three. And then opened my eyes to find myself in the recovery ward with tubes hanging from several parts of my body. It was a strange feeling to realise that two hours of my life had disappeared forever — hopefully along with the tumour — in what seemed like just a few seconds. I felt sure that this invasion of my body was now all over and after a couple of days in hospital recovering I would be free from this growth so I could get on with my life.

It turned out that the two-hour operation had removed most of the growth, but a magnetic resonance imaging (MRI) scan shortly after the operation showed that the surgeon was not able to remove all the cancerous cells and further treatment would be required. The scan also showed that my thyroid was also potentially cancerous, although this was difficult to prove. Dr Tim told me that if the thyroid turned out to be cancerous it too would have to be removed.

Oh great, I thought, *more bloody surgery.*

Anne was staying with me for a few weeks and we waited nervously for the final results of the surgery. The tumour, along with the MRI scan, was sent to Royal Brisbane and Women's Hospital for further examination. Dr Tim said that he was sure that I would need intensive treatment to destroy any remaining cancer cells. This would most likely mean radiotherapy and perhaps chemotherapy. The thought of such invasive therapy filled me with horror.

Dr Tim said he wanted me to see a special group of doctors who meet every Friday at the hospital to examine neck and throat cancer patients and recommend appropriate treatment.

I had a week or so at home before the meeting with the committee, and I used the time to look inwards to assess the best solutions to my situation. I did many deep meditation sessions and also connected with my spirit advisors with whom I had been working in writing my books. I also remembered that the spirit doctors who work through the healer John of God in Brazil never attempt to interfere with mainstream medicine, but work in harmony with medical practitioners. Having had several contacts with them through John of God in New Zealand in 2006 and in Brazil two years later, I was not surprised when a clear message came through from them in my meditations telling me to undergo radiotherapy (for more information, see www.johnofgod.com).

Feeling more than apprehensive, I drove the two hours from home to the hospital for more scans before my meeting with the head and neck committee, which comprised many different medical specialists and therapists. The day before I met with them I had to have another PET scan. The committee used these images as part of their findings.

Anne had to return to Sydney because of prior commitments and my son Matt came with me on the big day. It was shaping up to be a daunting experience. Once the dreaded 'C' word starts getting bandied around, it's enough to make anyone nervous. We were admitted to a waiting room with another twenty or thirty people, who were all meeting with the committee. Most of them were senior citizens and sat with a family member or friends trying to look calm. My heart went out to an elderly man, frail and clearly aged in his eighties, who was obviously alone and looked very lost as he faced the ordeal without a shoulder to lean on for support. And there was an older lady who sat forlornly in a corner of the waiting room with her loneliness wrapped around her like a cloak. I silently gave thanks for Matt's support.

We were all looked after by a friendly and supportive group of practitioners, who were obviously accustomed to dealing with all kinds of emotions. The clinic is very thorough. Each patient sits in a private room and is visited by a variety of specialist medical practitioners — oncologists, ENT specialists, radiotherapists, psychologists, dentists, dieticians and even a social worker to help with diagnosis, information and to recommend future arrangements.

I was doing my best to keep an open mind about mainstream medicine. Certain members of my family were surprised I had even come this far down the conventional road, assuming I would choose an alternative route. I think they feared that I would head off to some remote mountaintop, grow a beard, do a lot of soul-searching and eat only raw vegetables for my cure. I must admit it was a tempting thought.

By the time I headed off to Brisbane to meet the committee, I had almost resolved in my mind to accept my spiritual advisory team's advice and take the radiotherapy option, which I was told would be the likely recommendation. I did wonder whether I had folded and given in too easily when faced with the consequences of cancer. My spiritual team assured me that I would be able to combine this treatment with many spiritual and alternative methods that would present themselves along the way. However, my intuition kicked in and alarm bells rang again when it came to the question of chemotherapy. So I dug my heels in and resolved that nothing anyone said would convince me to undergo chemotherapy, a decision which I made clear to the two oncologists who examined me. My research into chemotherapy and its effects had filled me with dread and I was determined to stand my ground. One of the doctors was a specialist in chemotherapy and did not seem too impressed with my resolution. In fact she looked quite irritated. *But what the hell*, I thought, *it's my neck*.

Each specialist prodded and peered as they examined my throat and neck and then came forth with what seemed at the time like a mountain of information to digest. Thank heavens Matt was taking notes and I had remembered to bring my audio recorder. I knew that in the intensity of the day most of the details would go in one ear and out the other, and I am not someone who remembers medical stuff easily at the best of times. As the morning progressed, I also consulted with an ENT specialist, a psychologist, a dietician and the hospital patient advisor. All in all it was a very thorough and professional procedure.

After seeing all the patients in each week's group, the committee retires in jury fashion to consider its multiple verdicts. Meanwhile the patients take an hour or so to calm their anxieties and attempt to eat some lunch as they await the verdict. I think I managed a sandwich and a coffee in the hospital cafeteria, although even at the time I couldn't have told you what was in the sandwich. As I sat munching, Matt and I agreed that the head and neck committee with its dedicated specialists is a wonderful service provided for public patients and deserved high praise. I felt fortunate to be getting the benefit of their combined wisdom.

Once a consensus of opinion has been reached, an oncologist is appointed to work with each patient. I had struck a rapport with one of the oncologists who examined me and hoped she would be assigned to my case. Back in my small consulting room after lunch, I held my breath waiting for the committee's verdict. I was surprised when a youngish looking man entered the room and identified himself as Dr Charles, saying that he would be working with me as my oncologist and case officer. This was the first time we had met and I wondered why it was decided he would be my treating specialist. He was softly spoken and a thoroughly delightful man. We soon struck up a rapport and I felt the start of a comfortable relationship. We immediately agreed to call each other by our first names so I knew this was not going to be a rigid and formal doctor/patient association.

Charles was joined soon after by another doctor, an ENT specialist, an imperious and very brusque man around sixty years of age, who sat looking bored as Charles told me of the committee's findings. 'Dr Charm' then chipped in and coldly informed me that I had a squamous cell carcinoma and stated that my cancer was the result of HPV, or human papillomavirus, and sexually transmitted. He gave me no further explanation and I was left to let my imagination run riot. I blusteringly informed him that I am heterosexual as his implication indicated otherwise. He said that this wasn't important, but did not offer any further explanation. All sorts of images and memories crowded into my thoughts, as I struggled to come to terms with the offensive way he delivered his information. Over the years I have had my fair share of adventures with the fair sex, but was in a long-term monogamous relationship with Anne, which made me question his diagnosis. Not only that, my son Matt was in the room with me, which made the whole scenario quite embarrassing for the both of us.

I felt very affronted by his haughty, dismissive attitude and presumably was expected to do my own research about this HPV virus because he just looked away after delivering his verdict like some judge in a murder trial. Fortunately he proved to be the only doctor who ever made me feel uncomfortable during the entire treatment and I never saw him again, thank heavens. A staff member later told me he was like that with everyone and a very unpopular man as a result. A year or so after my treatments finished, I had a consultation with a different ENT specialist, who was much younger and more understanding about this diagnosis. He told me that the latest findings about HPV reveal that most of us have it as part of our physical make-up and limiting any cancer catalyst to sexual transmission is a very out-dated finding. Interestingly, while writing this book I found some official medical information that indicated this old-school doctor's automatic diagnosis of HPV was indeed very narrow minded, as it excluded other potential catalysts for this form of carcinoma. Full details are included later in my story.

My head still pounding from this offensive doctor, I waited for Charles to let me know the final verdict of the committee. Fortunately the other doctor having done his best to spoil my day, got up and left without another word. *Thank God for small mercies*, I thought.

My own ENT specialist, Dr Tim, had earlier told me he thought they would recommend a six-week period of treatment, which left my head spinning at the time. When Charles told me that I would have to undergo *seven* weeks of radiotherapy, I felt the blood drain from my face.

Seven long weeks, thirty-five doses of radiation pumped into my neck and throat. *Bloody hell!* I thought, and probably voiced my reaction as well.

However Charles did say that because I had never smoked and was a modest imbiber of alcohol, there was an 80 per cent chance that radiotherapy to the carcinoma in my throat would provide a long-term cure. When I asked him what that meant to my lifespan he said, probably fourteen or fifteen years. I decided I was happy with that prognosis and that I could achieve everything I wanted in that time. Charles explained that it didn't necessarily mean that I would die from a recurrence of cancer, which I later took to mean that, as I would be in my early eighties by then, it was probably the average lifespan for a male. Then again, can anything be guaranteed medically?

I told Charles that I was concerned that radiotherapy would damage my throat and prevent me from doing any more broadcasting work. This very gentle and caring man told me that because of the technology available at the Brisbane hospital he was sure he would be able to avoid the sensitive vocal areas in my throat and that my voice would be fine.

My gut reaction was to completely trust Charles, as deep down I knew that he was being genuine, and not simply offering token reassurance just to get me to sign the consent form. He explained that the radiotherapy process he would be using in my case is called tomotherapy and is able to be micro-tuned by computer settings to select areas being treated. He could program the area to avoid my vocal chords and lymph nodes and to have minimal impact on my salivary glands. As the Cancer Centre of America describes the tomo process on its website, 'With this advanced technology, we can sculpt powerful and precise radiation beams to treat hard-to-reach tumors. Using built-in CT scanning to confirm the shape and position of the tumor before each treatment, TomoTherapy reduces radiation exposure to healthy tissues and organs.'

At the time of my treatment only three hospitals in Australia had installed tomotherapy machines: in Brisbane, Sydney and Townsville in North Queensland. By mid 2016 tomotherapy has been installed in two other locations in the country. It was my good fortune to be admitted to this program. Certainly my voice could still be affected, as the cancer being treated was dangerously close to my vocal chords, but the other machines in use target a wider area and would certainly have caused problems. I had originally been thinking of going to a hospital much closer to home, but when Dr Charles explained the benefits of tomotherapy I soon abandoned that idea.

He also told me that the radiotherapy would have certain side effects, which I had to nervously accept as he detailed them. During treatment and for a healing period of at least six months, I could expect my taste buds to be blasted, dry mouth syndrome would be most likely to occur as the salivary glands are affected, my energy levels would be all over the place and, most significantly, I could expect to have a very sore throat as the treatment progressed. Apparently some people have such painful throats they find difficulty in swallowing, and a few even have to have a tube placed into their stomach so they can be fed. I also had to have a dental assessment because the radiation would affect my jaw and could create ongoing dental difficulties.

Being born under the astrological sign of Cancer, I enjoy my food, but the thought of having a tube inserted into my stomach made me feel instantly nauseous. I wasn't sure how I would achieve it, but I determined not to let that happen to me.

This was all head-spinning information, but I was determined not to back out once I had made the decision to have radiotherapy. I was happy to trust in the information and guidance that I had been given. A positive aspect was that the committee had respected my determination to reject chemotherapy. I must admit I was preparing for a battle and was relieved when the issue did not arise.

I was thankful that Matt was at the wheel of the car as I had a lot to think about during the peak-hour drive back to his house where I was staying the night.

Back home the next day I recorded my telephone conversation with Anne, who was now back in Sydney. She asked how I felt after speaking with Dr Charles and the other specialist who was with him. Listening to the recording I chuckle as I write these words, because my reply said it all. 'I was absolutely f***ing shattered.'

3

Preparing for Radiotherapy

Many years ago, when I needed some help with a perplexing situation, I was introduced to the rune stones. Over the last three decades or so I have benefitted from the incredibly accurate messages that can be received by consulting the runes. Far from being some weird and way-out source of self-communication, these small flat stones have been around for centuries. Runes, which were widely used by the Vikings and were part of the ancient alphabet used in northern Europe, each bear a symbol that has its own special message when drawn from the bag that contains them. They are essentially a way to access your own inner wisdom. Many people find the feedback they receive from using them is invaluable.

My method is to focus my mind on whatever concerns me at the time and then mentally ask, *what do I need to know about the situation at hand?* I then close my eyes, put the fingers of one hand into the rune bag, scrabble my fingers through the stones and let a rune find its way into my fingers. Consulting the runes has always been unerringly accurate for me, and the messages I have received over the years have helped me shape my life. I can honestly say that I have never received a message that did not answer my question.

Still feeling very shaken up a few days after arriving home, I grabbed my bag of runes to see what message I needed to know. I drew the stone called Kano, which is described as 'the rune of opening up, of renewed clarity'. As it was reversed, or in an upside-down position when I drew it, I looked for the appropriate part of the message contained in *The Book of Runes*. I have interviewed its author Ralph Blum and have every faith in his interpretations, which have served me well over the years.

Once again Ralph's explanation came up with the goods. I could hardly believe how appropriate the text was to my situation. The message described 'an aspect of myself that was dying that was no longer appropriate or valid'. It called for giving up the old and preparing to live for a time empty, and called for developing inner stability. This described in a nutshell what I was going through. It went on to say that 'failure to face up to the death of part of myself would constitute a loss of opportunity. It is important not to be seduced by the momentum of old ways while waiting for the new to become illuminated in its proper time.'

I was not surprised that the message hit the mark. I sat back for a few minutes to take it all in and contemplate what it meant for me at this stage.

I realised immediately that *death* represented the blackness within me that had manifested as cancer, which had to be removed. It was an *opportunity* and not some kind of punishment that I had to suffer. The mist slowly started to clear from my mind.

A couple of days after I arrived home, Dr Tim contacted me to say that the committee had also examined my thyroid report, which revealed a 60 to 70 per cent chance of cancer on the right side of the thyroid. It would have to be removed as soon as possible because, if surgery was required at some future date after radiotherapy, potentially the long-range repercussions would be far more serious.

Tim then told me he had booked me in for hemi-thyroidectomy surgery in a couple of days, whereby the right half of my thyroid would be surgically removed. If subsequent tests proved it was cancerous, the left side would probably also have to be removed soon after. This left little time to come to terms with another hospital visit.

So two weeks after my first surgery, it was back to the same hospital for round two on the medicine wheel. The operation took about two hours and when I was being wheeled back to the recovery room with a fuzzy head and the inevitable tubes dangling from all directions, my heart lifted when I saw the face of my son Matt in the corridor. After I settled into my hospital bed we managed to have a lovely conversation which kick-started my healing process. That night was far from restful, as I battled with the after-effects of the anaesthetic, all the time trying to avoid getting tangled up in the tubes that seemed to sprout from everywhere at the same time. Anyone who has been in hospital will remember being dragged out of their slumber at about 6 am to have various medical procedures thrust at them as they try to focus on the new day. This is usually followed by some form of breakfast, whether you are ready for it or not. Half expecting hospital jelly for breakfast after a throat operation, I was relieved when it was not on the menu. I was in the recovery ward waiting for my private room to become available, dreaming longingly of bacon and eggs once I escaped the hospital regimen.

My reverie was rudely interrupted when the patient in the bed opposite hauled out his mobile phone and started to launch into a business call at about 7 am. From the size and sound of him, he was obviously in the building industry and loudly issuing instructions for some project he was working on. Still recovering from my operation (and breakfast), I was far from impressed when he started to make another intrusive phone call, so I let him know in no uncertain way how I felt about his lack of concern for the other patients in the ward. He became quite angry and for a moment I thought as he jumped out of bed he was going to come over and thump me. But instead he just snarled an insult at me and went into the corridor to continue his commercial activities. The other patients gave me approving nods, and a few minutes later I was wheeled out of the ward and into my own room. Fortunately I never saw this loud-mouthed boor again. I don't think he was accustomed to being challenged. I felt sorry for the poor tradesmen who worked for such a rude individual.

I spent the next couple of days quietly recovering before being released back into the wild to await the next stage of my medical adventure. It only took a few days before Dr Tim rang with the news that, because the right side of the thyroid was definitely cancerous, it would be best if he whipped out the remaining bit, just to be on the safe side.

'Not another bloody operation,' I replied. 'What about the radiotherapy? I thought they want to get started on me as soon as possible.' However Tim was adamant that he had to get into my throat again with his scalpel and booked me in for operation number three on the day before Good Friday. *What a fun way to spend Easter*, I thought, feeling a little sorry for myself. I had plans that didn't include surgery and hospital food.

Just to add to the occasion I had a carcinoma skin cancer about the size of a ten-cent coin on my breast bone that had to be excised, so Dr Tim said he would throw that in as a bonus. Happy Easter!

I had some misgivings about the second thyroid operation because I felt intuitively that it was not cancerous. The dilemma in these delicate cases is whether to trust your intuition or play it safe? By now I was so far into the hospital frame of mind I decided, albeit reluctantly, to forgo the Easter bunny for operation number three.

Back at the hospital only four weeks after the first operation, I was now on first names with several of the staff. I was even able to call the anaesthetist by his nickname as he prepped me for surgery. 'If this keeps up I'll be on the payroll here,' I mused. Tim's colleague Dr John decided he wanted to be part of the action as well, particularly for the skin cancer removal, which was in a tricky spot on my breast bone with not much skin to be able to stitch.

When I woke up with more of the obligatory dangling tubes, my daughter Bec was by my bedside, despite having put in a long day's work at the university where she worked as a psychologist. It's always wonderful to see someone you love at times like these. Maybe Easter wouldn't be so bad after all. When my eldest granddaughter Isabella came to visit the next day with one of her friends, it put the icing on the cake for me.

The hospital staff were wonderful and even gave me an Easter egg before I managed to escape home after lunch on the Sunday. By now my body was getting accustomed to being sliced and diced and it healed rapidly after the Easter onslaught.

I was given instructions to take it easy and let nature take its course before the next onslaught. The trouble with that is the mind starts to work overtime and 'taking it easy' is not so easy after all. Sitting around doing nothing has never been my cup of tea, and the days tended to drag. But I had discovered the books of Bernard Cornwell. I enjoy reading historical novels so this, along with presenting my internet radio program, helped keep my mind active.

I had mixed feelings when the tests came back a week later showing the second part of the thyroid was indeed benign. On one hand, my intuition turned out to be spot-on but I was now thyroid-less. I would have to take thyroxine tablets every day for the rest of my life — not a happy thought for someone who dislikes taking pharmaceutical medication at the best of times.

Because I underwent three major surgeries in only four weeks, I had to wait another couple of weeks for my radio-therapy program to begin — a good opportunity to get myself spiritually and mentally prepared for what I knew was going to be something of an ordeal. I also had a chance to stockpile a bunch of radio programs to be broadcast when I would be receiving treatment.

By now I was meditating daily and was reassured by my spiritual team that I would be looked after, so it came as no great surprise when I was offered the loan of a crystal-light bed in my home for the duration of my treatment. These beds were developed by John of God. By way of explanation:

Each bed has seven extremely clear and highly polished Vogel cut quartz crystals suspended approximately twelve inches [30 cm] above the client lying on a massage table. Each of the crystals has been cut to a specific frequency. Each crystal is aligned above one of the seven human energy centres, or chakras. Coloured lights chosen to match the colour frequency of chakra colours, radiate light and energy through the crystals to each respective chakra, and shine on and off in certain rhythms to cleanse, balance and align your energies. [see www.johnofgodcrystalhealingbeds.com]

It just so happened that because of power problems at the Australian Casa, the crystal bed was unable to be used there at the time: the Casa is a healing centre which is directly connected to John of God in Brazil and with which I am associated. I was more than grateful for this gift, which I believe was no coincidence. I knew I would be able to use the crystal bed to help my body to quickly and easily heal from the three major operations and from my future medical treatments.

Howard Toose, one of the dedicated members of the Australian Casa, and a guide at the Brazil Casa, travels around various parts of New South Wales giving crystal-bed healings. Howard told me that in recent years he has helped many people about to undergo cancer treatment. He said even those who had to have chemotherapy found that by using the crystal beds, the effects of their treatment were far easier and less painful than expected. Some people may explain this away as the power of the mind, or a placebo effect, but I strongly disagree.

I had already had a spiritual operation in Brazil in 2008, which saw a dramatic improvement in my eyesight. Thousands of other people have also had miraculous physical healings from John of God so, as far as I am concerned, the placebo effect does not come into it. For those interested in crystal-bed healings, there is more information available online, including

YouTube demonstrations, lists of practitioners and locations around the world, and a dedicated Facebook page.

I started having regular crystal-bed sessions soon after being released from hospital and found that my recovery from the three operations went smoothly and was pain free. My only legacy was a very dramatic propeller-shaped scar where my skin cancer was removed — at the time the nurses said it reminded them of a nunchuk, the weapon used by ninjas in Japanese action movies. I wore it like a badge of honour but, with the help of the crystal bed, the scar began to fade slightly.

I later ascertained that the nurses were far from experts in ninja weaponry, which other patients will probably find a blessing. What they referred to as a nunchuk was really called a three-pointed throwing star. Whatever the correct terminology, I still have my ninja badge of honour, which to me is far more acceptable than some ugly tattoo.

As the next few weeks passed, I discovered that the crystal bed was just the beginning of my spiritual preparation. I am fortunate to know and have worked with several excellent energy healers in the last decade or two. I was offered everything from distance healing to hands-on energy balancing from my good friend Glenda Anderson, who I originally consulted as a kinesiologist many years ago, but whose skills now extend way beyond that modality. Glenda helped me after my first operation to 'balance my meridians', which had been affected by the surgery. Then she gave me further healing sessions during and following my radiotherapy treatment, with very obvious effects.

Sonia, a lovely spiritual energy healer who had helped me on many occasions while I was living in Sydney, was having severe health problems of her own but still found time to send me healing energy from afar.

Howard Toose, who was leading a group to Brazil, offered to take a photo of me to John of God and ask for some long-distance healing from the spirit doctors who help thousands of people each year at the Casa de Dom Inacio. Photos of people needing help are placed in the entrance to the Casa and the doctors miraculously provide healing from afar. Some people might find this too way-out to accept, but my experiences of people being helped this way proves otherwise.

Support just flowed in from all directions and dimensions, most of it without me even asking for it. I think my guardian angel must have been working overtime to get me so much assistance. I also received healing energy from a spiritualist church group in Sydney and even had a whole congregation pray for me in a church near where I live. I play tennis with Graham, the pastor of the church, and was delighted when he asked if I minded if they prayed for me. 'Go for it,' I said. 'I'll accept all the help I can get.' My good friend Bob Murray, who is a wonderful medium living in Canada, also sent healing across the waters. Bob passed away in 2015 and I will be eternally grateful for his friendship and support.

The medium Marcia McMahon, who is also an artist and author and lives in the USA, contacted me to say that, 'I have someone called Judy coming through to me from the afterlife, who is very concerned for your health.' Judy is my late partner, who passed over in 1997 and has worked closely with me from the world of spirit on my books. Marcia had not read my books, nor did she have a clue who Judy was, which made the message all the more meaningful for me.

I also received a lot of help from Cancer Council NSW, the state body set up to help those going through treatment. They are dealing with people suffering a lot of mental and physical anguish, and it takes special and dedicated staff to deal with the many sensitive situations that arise. They told me that, as well as financial assistance to help with travel and accommodation costs in Brisbane, they would arrange for someone who had undergone radiotherapy for throat cancer to contact me so I could go through the procedures and ask for advice.

Unfortunately, as gently spoken and well intentioned as he was, my contact only succeeded in alarming me, as he had gone through a very harrowing time during his treatment about ten years earlier. He told me that it had been a very painful experience. He could not swallow and had to have a tube, or peg, inserted into his stomach so he could be fed. During the last two weeks of his radiotherapy, he had to do two sessions a day, which had a very bad effect on him physically and emotionally. To cap it off, he described in dramatic detail being fitted with a large mask for the procedure, which was bolted in place so he could not move for around twenty to thirty minutes during each treatment.

When I put the phone down after talking to him, my hand was shaking and my head was spinning. I wondered what the hell was in store for me during these seven weeks. I recorded my reaction at the time and said it made me feel 'stomach churningly ill'. There was a strong temptation to take flight and disappear — anywhere! I did have enough frequent flyer points to get to South America, but my intuition told me it was no good going back to John of God in Brazil. I needed to stay and face the music here.

While I was contemplating another journey to the John of God Casa in Brazil, my mind went back to my contacts with Joao de Dios, or John of God as he is popularly known in English-speaking countries.

He travelled to New Zealand in 2006 and did a three-day event at Lower Hutt, just outside Wellington. Anne and I decided to join the many Australians who crossed the Ditch, aka the Tasman Sea. Several people I had worked with in the metaphysical area in Sydney had told us about this South American healer, and I felt a strong pull to experience the effects he might have on my life. I was running a spiritual development group in Sydney and one of the members brought along a man who had been to Brazil and, after having a healing from medium Joao, discovered his cancer had been arrested. This clinched it for us, so we booked our flights and headed for Wellington.

That first day I joined the line of people queuing to see the enigmatic figure. He was clad in white and looked like some kind of revered religious leader. When it came my turn to stand in front of him, my request was read out in Portuguese — he speaks no English. Without really thinking too deeply, I simply asked if I could 'release the past and have a fresh start'. He looked at me and with a wave of his hand told me to join the afternoon group for a spiritual healing.

This I did, and like everyone else was told I had to rest quietly for twenty-four hours and then could not drink alcohol, eat spicy foods and pork or have sex for the following forty days. This seemed a bit strange, but I figured it was all part of the deal. Anne decided she didn't need a healing — she just wanted to observe the proceedings and be part of the meditation process that is an integral part of all Joao's healings.

We returned home to Sydney a few days later, and within a week I started to see my request to release the past manifest itself. I broke out into severe eczema, which in a few days had covered about 80 per cent of my body. I soon found out that you have to be very careful what you ask for in these circumstances.

My body eventually returned to some semblance of normality through a combination of natural treatments from my next-door neighbour Ian White, the man who brought Australian Bush Flower Essences to the world, together with a special diet, crystal-bed therapy, hands-on energy healings and many weeks of pain and discomfort. More than ten years later I still get outbursts of eczema, particularly when I do a past life regression, which most likely means I haven't fully released my past. Just how many past lifetimes require clearing I am not sure. However, I do wish to complete the process in this incarnation before heading back to the afterlife. I've obviously brought back enough karma to resolve into this incarnation.

Two years later I received strong spiritual messages from my guides to join a group of nine Australians heading for Brazil to John of God's Casa de Dom Inacio in the state of Goiás. This was to be a three-week stay, which would involve physical, emotional and spiritual healing according to the needs of each person. Mindful of my past experience, I had decided to ask for further healing for my eyes, having been born with an astigmatism in my left eye, and also to ask for spiritual guidance and future direction.

The first morning, joining the line for those who had received a healing in the past, I shuffled patiently along to see the great man again. As I got closer, I saw that he was sitting in a large comfortable throne-like chair as people consulted him one by one. In each session medium Joao incorporates one of thirty-three different spirit entities who speak and heal through him. Sitting on Joao's left was a beautiful woman who I later discovered was Dorothy, a retired opera singer who helped him to maintain the energy needed to sit in spirit for several hours at a time.

When it came to my turn I was expecting the few words that everyone received, whether it was to go and sit in meditation or to come back later for a spiritual operation. However, after my request was delivered, he looked directly into my eyes and told me to go and sit in a chair next to Dorothy. I was instructed to sit quietly, open my heart and focus on what I needed to do from now on with my life.

Surprised and slightly bewildered, I stepped onto the small stage and sat down. After I managed to settle my racing thoughts, I opened my heart chakra and focused my mind. And then the tears began to flow.

An energy I had never felt before that moment flowed through my entire being, as the tears flooded down my cheeks. It was like an infusion of spirit. This energy download continued until the end of the session. Time stood still for me and I had no idea how long I sat there (I later worked out it was nearly two hours). Looking back, it was one of the most emotional experiences I have had as I really went very deep and explored the inner reaches of my self, probably for the first time ever.

Afterwards, I emerged blinking into the sunlight and was given a bowl of the soup that is provided for all those visiting the Casa. The vegetable soup and a slice of dry bread helped ground me as I gradually came back to earth. Sitting on my own away from the other members of my group, I went over the events of the morning in my mind.

Why me? I mused. *Of the hundreds of people who went for healing that day, why was I selected to sit in the direct energy of the spirit entity, and what will happen next?*

The following day I was directed to have a spiritual healing for my eyes later that afternoon. I was still wearing trifocal glasses at all times, even after the New Zealand visit.

I sat in a crowd of people as Joao went through a group healing ceremony, and surprisingly I did feel a buzz of energy but nothing remarkable. Despite this, in the days following, my eyes slowly became much clearer and soon I was able to ditch the trifocals, and now only require reading glasses. My left eye straightened noticeably.

During the second week I joined the line to see Joao again, I presumed to get a clearance after my operation the previous week. This time, after passing by him and being waved away to join the meditation groups, I was suddenly called back by the interpreter amid puzzled looks from the people in the queue behind me. I was told that the title of 'filo de casa', a son of the house, had been conferred on me, a rare honour I later discovered. I was also asked if I would like to purchase some very special crystals from the mine where the Casa was situated. I figured to warrant this attention I must have done something right when I sat on the stage the previous week.

The next morning my crystals arrived, specially wrapped and handed over by Joao's chief assistant. He explained he was giving me two different crystals, with a male and a female energy. When meditating I was to hold the mother crystal in my left hand, as this resonates with the female side of the body. The crystals, which stand about 15 or 16 centimetres high and each weigh around a kilo, are very powerful and he instructed that I must keep them covered at all times in public. Nobody is to be allowed to ever see them, and when I pass away a trusted member of my family is to return them to a lake, deep river or the sea bed.

As I was handed them I felt a real buzz. The energy of these crystals was palpable. Walking through the village back to my lodgings to secrete them in my room, I suddenly became the focus of attention of every dog for hundreds of metres around. There were dogs everywhere around the Casa and before this they had ignored me. Now suddenly I was the flavour of the month. They tried to jump up at me and I had to hold the crystals high as I shooed them away. I realised then this was a sign of the power of these amazing crystals.

The next day I was directed to sit at the front of the Casa a couple of rows from where Joao was seated, and to meditate for the entire session while I held my crystals. They were now tucked inside small cloth bags so nobody could see them. As I started to meditate, I received very clear instructions in my mind to raise my vibrations while meditating and to keep raising them as much as possible. As I did this for the remaining sessions at the Casa, I could feel that I was able to easily connect with some of the many different energies in the spirit world and receive their messages.

These messages and contacts have continued whenever I meditate with these crystals, and have resulted in many changes to my life. Not long afterwards, for instance, I was inspired and guided to write the first of my books about the afterlife.

As I came out of my reverie and back to the present moment, I wondered what would be the best method of treating my cancer. I was still having second thoughts about undergoing any further intrusive mainstream medical treatments, so I meditated with the crystals and the answers were given to me very clearly.

I was given definite instructions to combine mainstream treatment, in my case radiotherapy, with the complementary medicine, natural healing and spiritual practices that would become evident as I proceeded. I was also told that I would write a book about my experiences which would help others to come to terms with their cancer treatments.

As I accepted these spiritual guidelines my mind cleared, and for the first time I felt positive about the future and which direction I had to take.

4

Accentuating the Positive

Three weeks before the treatments were scheduled to begin, I was summoned to Royal Brisbane Hospital for what I was nervously trying to pass off as 'the mask-fitting ceremony'. I tried to laugh it off as auditioning for the title role in the *Phantom of the Opera*, but it was all just bravado. Deep down I was feeling very apprehensive. I am not normally claustrophobic, but the very thought of being locked into a mask was very different. I remembered reading Alexander Dumas' novel *The Man in the Iron Mask* as a young man and now I was about to experience my own version of this story. I had always wondered why Dumas' protagonist didn't choke to death as his beard grew in that hideous mask, but at least I knew I would not have to worry about that problem.

The initial procedure is strange, to say the least. As I lay there stripped to the waist on a tray, which is similar to getting a CT scan, two nurses proceeded to slop a warm, rubbery substance all over my face, neck and shoulders. They then massaged it all over to form a mould of my upper face and shoulders, leaving only a slit for my nose and eyes. This takes about ten to fifteen heart-pounding minutes and, once they are happy they have a perfect fit, they smother ice on the substance to make it set. This only takes a few minutes, but it is a weird sensation, like being encased in warm jelly and then feeling it harden as ice bags were pounded into each curve to help the mask set. Once finished, the nurses peeled the mould off gently and took it away, to do strange, secret mask-type things with over the next few weeks. I wondered what the final mask would look like on the big day and, more importantly, how I would react to wearing it.

I was left feeling a bit sticky, but mighty glad to breathe easily again as I washed off the gooey residue from my face and shoulders, grateful that this strange ritual was over. I described the procedure to my daughter-in-law Claire that night over dinner, and my two granddaughters Stella and Molly sat open-mouthed with shock and amazement.

As I looked at their horror-stricken faces, the first of my dark thoughts around claustrophobia kicked in. How would I be able to cope with a large face mask bolted down to prevent me from moving, for thirty-five radiotherapy sessions of around twenty minutes each? The nurses had told me that I would have to lie absolutely still on my back during the treatments, otherwise any slight movement could end up damaging the adjacent areas of my throat. That meant my vocal chords. I was told that it was also important not to even cough during the treatment — any movement of the face was a no-no. My mind started to swirl at the thought of these restrictions.

Having been subject to uncontrollable bouts of coughing for about the last twenty-five years of my life, especially first thing in the morning, I wondered how I would fare. Fortunately I have never smoked, but anyone with a smoker's cough would have real problems — and smoking is a proven cause of throat and lung cancer.

Lying on my back has always been difficult as it causes breathing problems, so I lie on my side in bed. When I tried lying that way as a test, my throat closed over, my breathing became difficult and my mind started to panic at the thought of those thirty-five treatments. Over seven hundred minutes. How will I cope?

I knew I had to do something positive, otherwise my fears would create problems. Once again I remembered the acronym for fear — False Evidence Appearing Real — and then meditated on the problem.

The solution was simple: hypnotherapy. I had been contacted only a few weeks earlier by Judith Richards, a hypnotherapist based in the mountains behind the Sunshine Coast. I had interviewed her for my internet radio program 'RadioOutThere' and we hit it off really well. Judith specialises in trauma relief work and has a very interesting and impressive background. I really liked her approach to healing, and indeed to life in general, and we both share a wacky sense of humour. My intuition told me to contact her straightaway, which was one of the better decisions I have made in this lifetime.

Judith was only too pleased to help and we set up an appointment. My brother Mike and his wife Shirley live on the Sunshine Coast and I was staying with them after the mask fitting for a few days R&R, so the timing worked out perfectly. I was also well accustomed to hypnotherapy, having had a very enlightening past life-regression session twelve months earlier with another therapist as part of the research for my book *No Goodbyes*. Hypnotherapy had also helped me move on from crippling migraine headaches several years earlier.

With the mask-fitting a distant memory, I drove to the property where Judith's practice is based, enjoying the sweeping views back to the coast from her rustic mountain hideaway. Any tensions I had brought with me immediately melted away as Judith greeted me with a big smile and a hug. I knew then that my decision to embrace hypnotherapy to help me prepare for my ordeal was the perfect choice. Another example of the fruits of meditation.

5

Taming the Mind

Having a past life regression via hypnotherapy is very different to using the technique as a healing modality. Many people associate hypnotherapy with a stage act, where the hypnotist gets people to do all sorts of crazy antics to entertain the audience. People love watching people bark like a dog or try to lay an egg like a chicken while under hypnotic suggestion. However, this is just the fluffy tip of the iceberg — there is a lot more to hypnosis than making audiences laugh at childish antics.

The power of the mind is important to me and two of my favourite beliefs are that *thought creates reality*, because everything begins with the process of the mind, and *what you focus on expands,* so if you have a problem, focus on the solution and not the problem itself. The universe will pick up your thoughts and send you more of the same, so choose wisely.

Judith explained how we program our subconscious minds with all sorts of fears and images, and these need to be reprogrammed so that we can face these fears and remove them. She specialises in the area of trauma, and has helped a lot of troubled soldiers returning from battlefields with all kinds of demons in their minds. Judith told me in a radio interview that trauma hypnosis is a totally separate therapy from such areas as addiction hypnosis.

Judith maintains that in extreme trauma work there are physiological factors involved: the person becomes overwhelmed with stress hormones, which means 'the person involved is always on fight or flight freeze, pumping out adrenalin and looking where the danger is coming from'. She referred to it as being 'never able to rest, which is a bugger of a way to live.'

Listening back to her words before my appointment, I resolved to make sure I did not allow myself to ever get to the stage of mental trauma and decided to deal with my fears by following Judith's guidance to the letter.

The great thing about hypnotherapy is that there is no pain involved, no needles or surgery required, no pharmaceutical drugs to take. You just have to relax and trust in the process. As a person who has been meditating for many years, the concept of relaxing the mind and going within is a natural practice. So Judith had no trouble getting me to the stage where she could communicate with my subconscious.

There were three main areas of concern for my forthcoming radiotherapy program. Firstly, the potential claustrophobic reaction to being strapped and bolted into a mask that covered my face, neck and shoulders. Secondly, the fear of breathing problems while lying flat on my back for over twenty minutes at a time. Then there was the thought of coughing and the problems that could cause as I was buried behind my mask. Good heavens, I really needed help.

Judith started by asking my subconscious mind several questions using a technique called muscle testing, which I had experienced when I had kinesiology therapy several years before and had ample proof of its authenticity. I recorded my reaction to this on my audio recorder as it really had a huge impact:

> I was absolutely staggered and horrified when my subconscious revealed that not only did I believe that I *deserved* this cancer, I also believed subconsciously that I equate my success with negative outcomes and I deserved to die. Consciously this was not the case, but the subconscious mind, of course, works at an entirely different level. So my subconscious was undermining all those positive vibes I was trying to create to build myself up.

Judith was unfazed by this revelation, and apparently it is a fairly common occurrence. She showed me how to muscle-test myself and then gave me a series of exercises and techniques to help me reprogram my subconscious if I needed to in the future. Over the next few weeks I was able to verify my abilities to muscle-test and found it a valuable tool.

Judith then asked me to relax and lie flat on my back and cover my mouth. I was able to easily relax and went deep into hypnosis. When she brought me back into full consciousness again, she asked me how long did I think I had been lying on my back?

'About fifteen or twenty minutes,' I replied.

'No,' Judith said with a wry smile, 'you've been there for an hour-and-a-half, lying on your back and breathing through your nose. I don't think you are going to have a problem.' I was absolutely stunned, an hour-and-a-half! Not only that, but during the entire time I had experienced absolutely no problems with my breathing. Judith later reminded me I had also spent the entire time lying flat on my back, without even having a pillow.

Judith's hypnotic techniques helped me overcome the feelings of dread I had about being strapped into a mask for long periods of time. She also gave me several trigger phrases I could use to help with any pain in my throat that might be caused by the radiotherapy. And she programmed some support messages into my subconscious to help with the healing process.

After a session that lasted about two-and-a-half hours, I left Judith's mountain haven full of positive thoughts for facing up to seven weeks of radiotherapy.

6

Visualisation Techniques

Arriving home full of confidence and looking forward to a few weeks' break until the radiotherapy treatments were due to start, I started a regimen of crystal-bed energy work a couple of times each day. I was fortunate to have the space to set up a dedicated area for the bed, downstairs and away from the upper main part of the house. I figured that creating a special healing area at ground level would have the benefit of containing the energy in the one space and isolating it from the daily routine of the home.

The easiest method is to use a massage table or a bed and align the seven crystals over the energy centres (chakras) of the body. These appropriately coloured crystals are situated on extendable arms attached to a pole, which looks something like a boom microphone, and are electrically powered. All I had to do each time was slide under the apparatus, cover my eyes, turn on some appropriate music and start the crystals on their healing duties. It's important to make sure the eyes were covered so that the blinking of the crystal lights do not interfere with the healing process. Most crystal-bed healing sessions run for at least thirty minutes but may go much longer, according to the needs of the person concerned.

Playing the right kind of music is important to help slip easily into a quiet meditative state of mind. Another vital step is to have an intention for a healing session in order to focus the mind in the right direction. In my case, on each occasion it was easy because I was simply preparing myself emotionally and physically for the radiation that was going to invade my body. I also asked for spiritual help and guidance to both prepare and protect me during the treatments.

All was proceeding happily until my mind started to play a few tricks with me. Up until this time, following my session with Judith I was able to lie on my back in complete comfort and easily slip into a meditation. However, because I knew I would not be able to move during the radiotherapy session, I decided to 'rehearse' and see how easy it would be to stay completely still for twenty minutes or more. This immediately turned into a problem. My throat suddenly dried up and I needed to cough, my nose itched, the bed was too hard … the list went on and on. I couldn't last for more than about five or six minutes without something making me move or change position on the bed. I thought to myself, *oh no, don't tell me all that good work with Judith has come undone.*

I gave myself several sessions to accustom my mind to this new situation, but the problem persisted. No matter how hard I worked to clear my mind or set positive intentions, a twitch, an itch or even a sneeze would decide to come and join in the mind games.

I confided the problem to my psychologist daughter Rebecca and asked for some advice. By now I was seriously worried about keeping perfectly still while the tomotherapy machine wacked radiation into my neck.

'It's easy,' she told me. 'When you lie down, do a full body relaxation exercise, starting at the crown of the head and going down to the tips of your toes, relaxing each area as you go. Then think lovely relaxing thoughts and visualise beautiful places to go. Then when you start your treatment, you can disappear into a different part of your mind. Just go to a peaceful place and relax.'

How bloody obvious was that? I had been meditating for more than twenty years and also conducted meditation groups and recorded meditation CDs, but the obvious solution had eluded me. I felt a little foolish — but very relieved — at her wise words. It proved to me how easy it is when we get stressed to let fear and worry conquer logic, positive emotions and even experience. At that point I had nothing to fear, but as US President Franklin D Roosevelt said in his first inaugural speech, 'the only thing we have to fear is fear itself.'

I couldn't wait to put Rebecca's advice into practice, and of course it worked like a dream. I have several sanctuaries I have created in my mind over the years to escape to during meditation and I visited each one to see where I felt most comfortable. It worked like a charm and I was able to 'rehearse' lying perfectly still to my heart's content.

However, during one meditation I received an intuitive message to forget the distant past and create a whole new set of visualisations which would be more suited to my purpose. So I started to visit a few favourite destinations where Anne and I had been to in recent overseas holidays and planned to return to in the future. Paris immediately jumped into my mind and I knew this was the way to go. Not only that, but I would save a bundle on air fares. We had stayed in Paris twice in the previous three years, sharing some wonderful experiences, and the thought of recreating some of my favourite memories made me feel really good. So each time I had a crystal-bed session I would arrive in Paris and revisit in my mind a memorable place or occasion. We always stayed on the Left Bank near the Latin Quarter and each day explored different parts of what is now my favourite overseas city. Galleries, historical sites, museums and of course restaurants soon started to come alive in my mind.

I also soon found myself once again strolling through the beautiful grounds of the Arthur Findlay College in Essex where Anne and I had done a week-long residential course in mediumship only a few months earlier. This turned out to be an integral part of each session once the treatments began.

I had also created a sanctuary in my mind when doing a personal development course many years ago, and have retreated there on many occasions to escape and reflect. So once again I returned to this inner tropical haven to sit out on the wide deck and gaze at the beach below.

These visualisations would give me plenty of scope to work with when the time came.

With this new discovery, I may have moved slightly while having my crystal-bed healings. I honestly don't remember, but it would only have been to squirm with delight at these absorbing images and memories.

7

Final Preparations

At first the thought of having a three-week window before heading to Brisbane to start radiotherapy felt like the calm before the storm. I knew the cyclone was on the way, but felt more and more confident about my mental and emotional ability to cope with its demands as the days counted down.

Not that I sat around doing lots of thumb twiddling and navel gazing — that has never been my practice anyway. As my treatments would be in Brisbane, I had to finalise my accommodation for the seven-week period. Living about two hours drive south of Brisbane, in northern New South Wales, it was not feasible to commute. Some sessions would start at 8 am while others would not be until late afternoon. The times were scattered like this to make it fair to everyone receiving treatment.

Dr Charles had warned me I could expect various side effects as the treatments progressed, including a significant loss of energy, so finding the right accommodation was imperative. As the treatments were only held on weekdays, I wanted to drive home for the weekends to rest and also, most importantly, to have two or three crystal beds each day.

I looked to my old friend Google and an extensive online search eventually turned up the perfect solution, a block of short-term self-contained apartments in Spring Hill, a charming inner city suburb. It was only a few minutes' driving time from the hospital, or a twenty-five minute walk if I felt up to it. The apartment block was surrounded by cafés and restaurants, an ideal place to repair to in between treatments. There was also a regular bus service which stopped at the front door and continued on to Royal Brisbane Hospital every half hour. A city loop bus also stopped right outside the front door and that would take me into the city centre to do my shopping and catch a few movies. I called in to see the manager when I was in Brisbane for some medical tests and was given a choice of several comfortable and spacious one- and two-bedroom units. Cancer NSW would pay part of the rent, which made all the difference and meant I could stay in comfortable surroundings away from the hospital and its environment and not break the bank; it also provided me with a car allowance. This, along with their very caring staff, took a great load off my mind in those few weeks.

By now the word had spread around my family and friends, and more and more support materialised each week. Sonia, my friend and spiritual healer, said she would send me healing energy during my treatments. My photograph went to Brazil with Howard Toose, who was taking a group to visit John of God. Howard told me later that he handed my photo to John of God and asked for distance healing on the very same day that I started my radiotherapy treatments. Coincidence? I think serendipity is a better description.

My friend Glenda Anderson gave me a healing session on one of the weekends I was home, and it helped balance a lot of the negative energy that was building in my body through radiation. To some people this may sound a bit way out, but I am a great believer in positive energy and am truly grateful to all concerned. We are all essentially energy beings attached to a physical body so we can have a human experience. Extreme medical treatments and conditions, as well as other challenging aspects of our lives, can have a huge effect on our spirit, which stays imprinted there after we pass away and return to the afterlife. So it is important to deal with these potentially negative effects as they occur and not let them become permanent fixtures.

On reflection I realise that it may seem as if I was throwing everything but the kitchen sink into my preparation. However, I made sure that all these spiritual and healing energies I was working with complemented the mainstream medical advice I was being given. For instance, I had to reluctantly stop taking vitamin C because Dr Charles told me it would interfere with the radiotherapy.

The Brisbane Dental Hospital contacted me for an appointment to check my dental health, as radiotherapy in the neck and throat area can have a dramatic effect on the jaw and teeth. Like most people I only go to the dentist when I have to. Not that I'm afraid of dentists, but there always seems to be something more important to do with my time. So it came as no great surprise to find that I had some urgent dental work to be done before I could hit the tomotherapy trail. Something else to make my heart beat faster.

The rest of the time I spent completing the final stages of the editing process on my second book, which I was determined to finish before the treatments began. Although I was confident the radiotherapy would be successful, I wanted to make sure there would be no potential hold-ups with the publication. My publisher decided to put the launch date back six months to early 2014, to allow plenty of time for any healing that I needed before the arduous publicity work associated with getting a book released. I was also busily pre-recording as many programs as I could for RadioOutThere to cover the period of my treatments. Fortunately, everything went very smoothly and fell into place with no apparent stress involved. Another good sign that I was on track, I told myself.

Through all of this, Anne was a tower of strength and her love helped me through some challenging times. She was still in Sydney when I started the treatments and would not be able to be with me for the first two weeks of radiotherapy. Anne had also been having a few health problems of her own and needed some recovery time. However, Dr Charles had told me the first noticeable after-effects of radiotherapy would only start in earnest from the third week onwards, so I was not concerned she would not be there in the initial stages. My son Matt and his family lived not far from the hospital if I needed help.

The day before I went to Brisbane to start the treatments the phone ran hot with messages of goodwill. My family and friends, of course, and my first wife Jann rang with best wishes. She had remarried and her husband David was a much loved and talented thoracic physician, a man who I greatly respected and admired. David helped me a lot when I was researching the question of radiotherapy, and they were both glad I had made the decision to have the treatments.

I was so grateful to hear from so many people, including my good friend Terry who was such a vital part of the development group I ran in Sydney for ten years. My voice-over agent Alex at EM Voices rang, as did the boys from Telstra where I had been recording voice messages for some fifteen years. My friend and former astrology teacher Garry Wiseman got in touch out of the blue to wish me well. He reminded me of the two people we both knew who had chosen to only treat their cancer with natural therapies, with fatal results. He was full of support for my decision to combine the mainstream with the spiritual and alternative. He talked of a well-known world figure who decided to use only alternative means to treat his cancer. Despite having the money to afford the best treatment on the globe, he did not survive. It was information like this that made me more and more confident, and not once did I have any fear of the treatment failing or of dying.

It occurred to me in those last few days before going to Brisbane that I had not told anyone except family and a couple of very close friends about my cancer, but the word seemed to spread despite this. I felt very blessed to have so many people in my corner.

After Judith's hypnotherapy removed the negatives in my mind, all manner of good things had started to happen, seemingly of their own accord, which made the future look very bright.

Suddenly my three-week period of grace had disappeared and I was on the road heading for Royal Brisbane Hospital, full of nervous anticipation.

8

The First Day

At first I thought it rather strange that my treatments were scheduled to begin on a Thursday, which meant that I would only have two sessions before going home for the weekend. My logical mind automatically anticipated that a new program would start on a Monday and proceed week by week from there in groups of five treatments a week.

But it was soon obvious that over time many people's programs had changed for various reasons and it was simply not possible to create a perfectly aligned roster for everybody. Actually it turned out for the best because I only had to turn up for two days and then I could flee back to my sanctuary for the weekend. Great!

I stayed with my family in Brisbane that first week and Matt once again accompanied me to the fateful first appointment at 3 pm on Thursday 9 May and my introduction to the Big T, as I had begun to think of the tomo machine. The first thing that struck me was how friendly and helpful the nursing staff was when I arrived. Not that you expect grumpy nurses and off-hand treatment, but loads of smiles and encouragement can do wonders for nervous hospital patients.

The radiation therapy section is a part of Cancer Care Services on the third floor of a wing of the Royal Brisbane Hospital, a giant complex comprising three main buildings linked by the inevitable maze of corridors. I presented myself to the reception desk with a crisp new appointment card which had been provided with only that day's date and appointment time on it. As I look at this card now, it is a battered and tattered version of its original self, an ongoing reminder of the thirty-five treatments it represents.

The friendly receptionist gave me some basic information about my treatment schedule and told me my appointment for the following day was at 8 am. *Good,* I thought, *that means I can be home before lunch and enjoy a nice long weekend.* I wandered over to the waiting room to nervously wait with Matt for my name to be called over the loudspeaker. After about ten minutes I heard, 'Barry Eaton, please go to LA5.' Matt gave me a little smile of encouragement and I apprehensively walked down two corridors to my first encounter with radiotherapy. Knowing that my son would be waiting when I emerged was a great comfort. My heart still pounded though as I walked around to LA5.

There, I had another wait while the patient ahead of me completed treatment, so I faced another finger-tapping five minutes sitting alone in the corridor outside the treatment room.

One of the important things you learn as an actor and presenter is always to go to the toilet before you go on stage or onto a film or TV set. There is nothing worse than being on stage and getting an urgent call of nature. Audiences don't react well to actors standing with their legs crossed! My early training paid dividends as I spotted a patients' toilet a few metres from where I was sitting, and I made a dash for it before I was summoned. More nerves? You betcha!

I had been told that if I would like to have some music playing during my treatment to bring an iPod which could be plugged into speakers adjacent to where my head was positioned. I had pre-programmed some lovely, relaxing meditation songs for the occasion from British performer Asha, one of my favourite musicians in this genre.

So when the radiologist finally came to collect me, armed with my iPod and my positive frame of mind, I walked into the treatment room and flashed her welcoming smile.

I thought of the old nursery rhyme: 'Come into my parlour said the spider to the fly.'

9

The Big T

'Okay, please strip down to the waist, leave your things on the chair, then come and lie on the bed. Make sure your phone is switched off.' This was the way each of my treatments would start.

As I lay on the bed with my head and shoulders carefully positioned in a specially made mould, a blanket was put over me — in case I got cold and started shivering, I suspected. One of the radiotherapists brought the head and shoulders mask and fitted it over me. This was the first time I had seen the finished article and was relieved to see it was made of mesh, something like a fencing mask. I would be able to see what was going on and could breathe through my mouth if I did have any breathing issues. Whew, what a relief.

The first fitting and finely tuned placement on the tomo sliding bed took a bit of time so I was able to get accustomed to the strange procedure I would have to undergo for the next seven weeks. It felt very weird as I was jiggled around on the bed into a final position before the mask was firmly clipped into place.

Two young-looking radiotherapists helped me to get settled and then the process of finely tuning the computer settings began. Because the tomo radiotherapy beam is so precise and operates with such micro settings, the adjustments are checked and re-checked before each session gets underway.

'It's very important that you stay perfectly still during the treatment. Any movement can cause problems.' I was staring at the ceiling through the mesh of my mask and the words came from somewhere beside me. When I asked what would happen if I started coughing or sneezing, I was told an automatic safety cut-off switch would be triggered. *Thank God for that*, I thought. The music from my iPod floated gently over me, producing murmurs of approval from the staff. Apparently some people choose very strange music to relax them. I asked if anyone brought rap or heavy metal? They just smiled indulgently and I was left wondering.

Feeling more and more like the *Phantom of the Opera*, I waited as they fine-tuned the computer settings. Now I was ready to go into the routine that I had been practising for weeks. Nerves jangling, I prepared myself for my first radiotherapy session and went quickly through the ritual that was to play such a significant part of my daily routine in the theatre. It worked like a dream, enabling me to sail through each subsequent treatment easily and free of stress. Looking back, I feel this routine played a significant role in my mental and emotional wellbeing in what for most people is a very stressful time.

As the therapists were standing next to me double-checking the settings, I closed my eyes and started my full-body relaxation exercise. Instructing my mind to calm down, I shifted my focus to the crown of my head and started to relax my body one step at a time. The head, then the face, neck muscles, into the shoulders, down each arm to the fingers, then I continued down the torso to the solar plexus, lower abdomen, down each leg, thigh, knees, calves and finally feet and toes. I relaxed each one in turn, breathing calm and peace into every part of my body. I also mentally created a cocoon of protection around my vocal chords, my lymph nodes and my salivary glands. These were the ultra-sensitive areas that could have been adversely affected by radiation and I was determined to prevent that, by positively using the power of my mind.

I was about halfway through the relaxation process, around the solar plexus region, when I heard one of the therapists say, 'Okay Barry, we'll be starting in just a minute.' My mind was so focused on my relaxation exercises that the voice seemed very distant. The bed slid into the machine as the radiologists left the room. I had reached the area around my feet when the Big T was up and running. By the time I'd finished relaxing my toes, my whole body felt calm and free of stress.

The whirring and beeping sound of the tomo machine was fairly quiet, unlike the clamouring and intrusive sound of an MRI machine. I thanked God for that small mercy.

Now I was ready to start part two of the relaxation routine I had planned, the visualisations. It was off to the Left Bank in Paris and firstly to the quaint Hôtel Bac where we stayed on our last visit. Using this as a base, I proceeded up the Rue du Bac towards the river Seine to visit my very favourite art museum, the Museé d'Orsay, which was about a ten-minute walk from our hotel. Here I wandered through galleries filled with some of my favourite painters — Van Gogh, Cezanne, Degas, Gauguin, Denis, Manet, Toulouse-Lautrec, just to name a few of the post-impressionists who I so admire.

I mentally calculated that this sightseeing had taken up a fair amount of my treatment time, so I quickly emerged back onto the Quai d'Orsay and wandered up along the banks of the Seine, stopping to watch some of the cruise vessels crammed with tourists as they took in the sights of the City of Love.

Still time to spare? Yes. The Big T was still whirring on relentlessly. Right, it was off to the Latin Quarter next to meander through the narrow streets and work out which restaurant to have dinner at that night. I was still immersed in my mind travels when Tomo abruptly stopped beeping and my bed slid automatically out into the room. Before I had time to say *merci*, the radiologist was loosening my mask and I emerged from my phantom-like reverie. I was back into what we laughingly call reality.

My twenty minutes of radiotherapy had passed quickly and easily and I felt no after-effects, so I determined to keep Paris in the schedule for all my treatments. I dressed quickly and went back out into the front room where Matt was waiting. He was relieved to see that I had a spring in my step and a smile on my face.

One down, thirty-four to go.

As I was having so many treatments over a seven-week program, I soon found that, as much as I love Paris I needed to expand my horizons. Before each visit to the tomotherapy room I would allow my intuition to guide me for that day's journey.

I ended up re-visiting other memorable places in France: Avignon, where I again enjoyed eating lavender-flavoured ice cream, and the mediaeval city of Carcassonne to feast on mouthwatering plates of the local dish, cassoulet. The further I went into my treatments, in reality the less appealing food was becoming, so I guess my mind decided this was the best substitute available.

Occasionally I just let my imagination take over and the music I was listening to determine the venue for the day. These mind travels took me to a few surprising locations.

I believe it doesn't matter where we choose to go in our visualisation — overseas, the beach or on a camping trip — it's up to the individual. The benefits of this exercise are invaluable in coping with the anxiety and nervous tension that everyone feels. Simply find or create your own sanctuary and retreat there to cope with any concerns you may have.

10

Early Days

My second treatment was bright and early the following day and I drove to the hospital in peak-hour traffic feeling much lighter and far more confident than the previous day. Knowing that my program of meditation and visualisation worked brilliantly on day one, I had not a care in the world.

The treatment was a breeze. Being the first patient for the day, there was no waiting around and I went into LA5 treatment room with only a slight increase in my heart rate. I was without Matt's support, so it did feel a little strange at first. But I knew I had to become accustomed to flying solo until Anne arrived.

The nurses and radiologists were just as friendly and helpful as the day before, so I knew they had not been putting on a front to ease my first-day nerves. My *Phantom* mask felt a little more comfortable and the sensation of being fastened firmly in place was not as daunting as the previous day. I soon slipped into my relaxation schedule and then disappeared off to Paris again as the Big T did its thing. This time I was enjoying an omelette and a croissant in our favourite bistro Le Terminus on Rue du Bac when suddenly it was all over and my tray slid out into the treatment room. I was almost sorry it ended so soon, as I didn't get to finish my croissant and coffee.

The great benefit of radiotherapy, I immediately discovered, is that there is absolutely no pain during the treatment. Even so, as I walked out of the front doors of the hospital after that second experience, I still had a slight feeling of relief, somewhat akin to escaping from the dentist after thirty minutes of drilling and filling.

By 8.45 I was out of the hospital and in my car leaving Brisbane on the way home. I turned on the radio, found a station playing a collection of hits and memories, and sang loudly as I hummed south down the highway.

If this was a taste of what radiotherapy was like, then all my apprehension and fears could be laid to rest. I was feeling very pleased with life for the first time in months.

Over the weekend I enjoyed all my normal activities, including three sets of tennis, along with several sessions on the crystal bed, which helped relax me even more.

The staff at the hospital had bent over backwards to help with my travelling situation and I was not due back until the following Monday afternoon. There was plenty of time for R&R and I took full advantage of it. By the time Monday came around I had plenty of time to prepare for the drive back to Brisbane and the start of week two.

Before beginning this lot of treatments, I checked into my new apartment block in Spring Hill and even had time to stock up with some provisions. I also had time to quickly explore the area. I discovered a couple of good restaurants and a great café in the next block, so things were looking better every minute. The medical staff told me that it is very important to make sure your time away from the hospital is in friendly, comfortable surroundings so you can relax in between treatments.

I discovered a lovely Thai restaurant in the same complex and enjoyed my favourite duck curry that night. My oncologist Dr Charles had warned me that, as the treatments progressed, I could expect to have a sore throat and would not be able to eat hot and spicy dishes for quite some time. Being a lover of curries, this was not the news I wanted to hear, so I thought I'd tuck into a few while I still could. Bad news for the Brisbane duck population.

By the time my treatment commenced at 4 pm I was settled in and ready for whatever the next five days would turn up. The second week went swimmingly, the treatments became easier every day. I was on top of the world as I drove back home the following weekend. I could hardly believe how quickly the week passed.

Week three began the same as the previous one, with an extra ingredient thrown in for good measure. I found out that each Monday I would have an appointment with Dr Charles, who would review my progress. On top of this, I would meet with the dietician before my first treatment of the week to help keep me on the straight and narrow.

Charles is a delightful man and we soon established a connection that made communication very easy. He asked whether I had experienced a sore throat yet, to which I replied, 'Not at all.' My first hint of apprehension came when he told me I could expect to have a sore throat before too much longer, as this was where the radiation was aimed and it was bound to have a reaction. He gave me a box of soluble painkillers to relieve the early symptoms and said I might need a more intense painkillers in future weeks. He also told me that I would probably have great difficulty in swallowing as we went further into the treatments, but the regular meetings with the dietician would put me on the right track. If necessary they could put a tube into my stomach and feed me that way. That little snippet of information rang a few alarm bells and made me sit up and take notice. Oops, there go those nerves again.

I put the painkillers in my pocket and wondered how long it would be before I would need the heavy-duty ones. I have a fairly high pain threshold, having come through many years of migraine headaches, so I wasn't too concerned at that stage. I had moved on from those crippling headaches with several sessions of hypnotherapy, and I figured that would be my fall-back position now. My hypnotherapist Judith had already volunteered to drive up to Brisbane to help me if things got too bad. Once again my wonderful support team was there for me, something that I would recommend to anyone going through cancer therapy. The more back-up you have, the easier things can be for you.

The week slipped by just as quickly as the last, with each day's treatment blending into the next. Matt, who works as a radio journalist at the ABC studios in Brisbane, came over for lunch on his way to work one day and was pleased to see that things were going well. However, as the week progressed, I began to notice a few changes were taking place. Was I just imagining it or was my throat starting to feel a little more tender? My taste buds also began to dine out elsewhere, and food started to taste more and more bland. I swallowed hard as I realised that after twelve treatments the easy times were now behind me.

The nursing staff told me to apply sorboline cream to my neck area, which was becoming increasingly tender. They said to expect things would get worse as the treatments continued, but that they would be there to help in whatever way they could.

I drove home that weekend still feeling pretty good, and my family came down from Brisbane to spend the weekend at my place. My daughter-in-law Claire prepared slow-cooked lamb on the Saturday night, one of my all-time favourite dishes. But after eagerly anticipating a lamb feast, I was shattered to realise it was almost tasteless for me. Food was resembling bland lumps of meat and vegetables and my neck and throat were starting to get more tender as the weekend progressed. I had been told that once the taste buds are affected, it can take months after the treatment concludes before they return to normal — or even approaching normal. Some food apparently can stay tasteless forever and spicy dishes are especially affected. Nevertheless, it was vital to keep eating, not only to keep up my energy levels but to ensure that I didn't lose too much weight. Apparently the face is the first place where weight drops off and that can result in the head moving inside the mask during a treatment, which of course could have a serious effect.

According to the medical staff, it becomes a mind-over-matter issue and the way to solve the problem is to remember what the dish tastes like while you are eating. I tried to use this technique but the lamb still tasted bland and I knew I was going to have to work a lot harder at the technique over the following weeks. The sad thing was I had absolutely no desire to go for seconds of one of my favourite dishes. Not only that, but the glass of red wine I had looked forward to had suddenly turned to vinegar. Yuk! Oh, my God, my life was being turned upside down.

Dr Charles had also warned that the radiotherapy would impact on my energy levels as the treatments progressed.

I would need to go easy on myself and not be afraid to have a rest during the day. *Hello,* I thought, *sounds like nanna nap times are on the way.*

Matt, Claire and my granddaughters Stella and Molly all pitched in and did some gardening work around my pool area, but it was as much as I could do to drag a few fallen palm fronds away before needing to sit down and rest. I felt like a 'real wuss' until I recalled Dr Charles's advice and retired to a deck chair.

Well, somebody had to supervise.

I drove back to Brisbane and stayed Sunday night with my family before heading back to the hospital the next morning for week four. Sore neck aside, I was looking forward to Monday as my lovely partner Anne was flying in that afternoon to be with me for the remainder of my treatments.

11

Anne to the Rescue

I had booked a larger apartment so Anne and I could enjoy our time in Brisbane. I settled into the new surroundings and then it was time to head back to the hospital for consultations with Dr Charles and the dietician. Dr C looked at my sore throat and, when I asked him if it was going to get worse, he said, 'I can't lie to you — yes, it is.' He told me to take soluble paracetamol as it made no sense to suffer pain, and then gave me a prescription for a morphine-based painkiller to use if things became really bad.

Afterwards I went in for treatment number thirteen, which meant that I was now more than one-third of the way through. Lucky thirteen I figured — only twenty-two to go!

Anne arrived late that afternoon and it was wonderful to see her again. Although we live in two different places for family reasons, we speak every day, but being together is altogether different. I had missed her birthday a few days earlier so we went out for dinner for a late celebration.

I decided to take the paracetamol before going to the Thai restaurant so that at least I would be able to swallow comfortably, even if I couldn't taste the food. However, my massamun beef dish was served in a rich sauce and, surprise, surprise, I could actually taste and enjoy it. The hospital dietician told me later that the secret to enjoying food during radiotherapy treatments is to use tasty sauces to make the food more palatable. I wasn't sure whether that extended to breakfast or not. Muesli covered in gravy didn't sound too appealing.

One of the other side effects of radiotherapy is the dry mouth and throat syndrome. Anne was quick to point out the next day that I had been snoring loudly, which of course I put down to the radiotherapy. Fortunately we had a two-bedroom unit, so that solved that little problem.

By now I had settled into a daily routine at the hospital and the tomo treatments were still painless, so each day came and went easily. The nursing staff gave Anne permission to come into the treatment room on her first morning to watch me as I was masked and strapped into place. She took a quick photo of me in situ before she had to leave so I could see an image of myself on the table. A very strange sight indeed.

Even though I was sailing through the daily treatments easily, by the end of that week my neck had become extremely sore. I later described it as being like a bad case of sunburn, and by this stage we were not quite at the halfway mark. There were still eighteen sessions to go.

The dietician recommended that I have protein dairy drinks to keep up my energy and weight, and my lovely daughter-in-law Claire arrived at the apartment with a box of coffee-flavoured milk drinks. But even though my neck was getting sorer by the day, surprisingly I was not having any throat problems, apart from dryness. Once again the dietician came to the rescue and suggested I start chewing gum — the chewing motion generates saliva. So here I was downing protein drinks and madly chewing gum each day, but it worked and that was the main thing. The crystal-bed therapy each weekend was obviously also helping. And I found out that ice cream is good for a sore throat, so that opened up a whole new world of possibilities as well. Soon a chocolate-coated Magnum or similar became a daily ritual, encouraged by the dietician. I felt like I was a kid again as I tucked into ice cream.

Emotionally I was feeling very positive, but was very glad that Anne was with me now that things were becoming more challenging. I also had a lot of support from family and friends with phone calls and emails coming in all the time, which was very comforting. I saw several people arriving at the hospital on their own every day, looking very lonely, and I wondered how they were able to cope. Although the nursing staff is very caring and supportive, it would be most difficult to go home to an empty house each day as the treatments progressed.

Now that Anne was with me, each day slipped by easily. The early winter weather was mild and we were able to go for a walk around the quaint suburb of Spring Hill. As we were only a few minutes from the city centre, we often took the opportunity to explore inner Brisbane and catch a daytime movie. My energy levels were not causing me any problems at this stage, although I also enjoyed quiet times reading and even the occasional nap.

My hospital appointments had fallen into a kind of pattern and we were able to plan each week accordingly. I started to feel a lot more familiar with the city of Brisbane and it was good to be out and about wherever possible to take my mind off the radiotherapy. I had seen some people just sitting forlornly in the hospital waiting room long after their treatment finished, almost as if they had no direction or even a place to go, and I was determined I would never just sit around and mope. Some people from out of town had fully subsidised accommodation provided. I was glad I was fortunate enough to be able to pay a little extra for an apartment so I could escape and not be constantly surrounded by sick people. I figured it was important to get away from the medical environment and lead as normal a life as possible.

The hospital staff was most helpful and each Friday I was given a very early time so I could slip away and head home for the weekend. What a wonderful feeling it was to walk in my front door each Friday, with no commitments and *just be*.

12

An Unexpected Visitor

Our second weekend at home was lovely and quiet, a walk on the beach on a sunny autumn Saturday followed by a restful Sunday, and of course several crystal-bed sessions. Eating was becoming more and more of a chore. This was a real challenge for a Cancerian, as we are notorious for our love of food — and drink. Anne was doing her best to think up and create appealing dishes so that I wouldn't fade away. However, I was very much overweight when I started the treatments, so there was no real danger of that.

Sunday morning provided a delightful surprise. I was slowly climbing my back stairs to the deck, my mind away with the pixies. Something made me look up just as I was about to reach out to open the gate. My hand froze in mid-air, stopping just a few centimetres away from grabbing hold of a very large snake which was draped over the gate and the adjacent railing. I don't know who got the bigger surprise, me or the snake, which then proceeded to slide gracefully up the back wall of the house.

I called out to Anne to bring her camera. I knew she would have been devastated to miss such a golden picture opportunity. Fortunately Anne is a good down-to-earth Taurean who is not afraid of snakes and spiders. She couldn't believe her eyes and rushed back inside for her camera.

Meanwhile I backed down the stairs and quietly came up another entrance to the deck. We both stood in awe of this beautiful creature. And then, instead of being scared off, our visitor turned around and glided gracefully along the railing of the deck and positioned itself comfortably in the morning winter sunshine, completely oblivious to the human occupants of the house.

Anne had a field day with her camera as our guest settled in for a Sunday sunbake, appearing completely at ease. I remembered that the pest inspector had told me earlier that year when he was performing his annual inspection that there was a large python skin in my roof. I must have looked a little concerned because he quickly explained that having a python, also known as a carpet snake, in your roof is very beneficial. They are not harmful to humans unless attacked, and they feed on rats and mice or other vermin. 'Every house needs a python,' he said cheerfully. I felt reassured but told him to leave the sloughed-off skin in the roof as I really didn't want a souvenir. What on earth he expected me to do with a second-hand python skin I can't imagine.

So now we had come face-to-face with our tenant in the roof and it measured around three metres in length, so there must have been a few vermin that no longer haunted my roof space. I decided to give our new friend a name. I didn't want to be completely obvious and call him Monty, so I opted for Percy. I like alliteration and Percy the Python had a good ring to it. We later discovered that Percy was in fact female, so that had to change to Persephone.

Our new friend made herself completely at home and allowed Anne to get quite close to capture her on camera. She even raised her head gently at one stage in a graceful pose. I could only guess that she is a Leo.

Percy stayed on the back deck peacefully resting for several hours. Then as suddenly as she had arrived, she was gone. I haven't seen her since, although I have heard her slithering about in the roof on a few occasions.

I later remembered that we were right in the middle of the Chinese astrological year of the snake, so Persephone's visit was very appropriate. Scott Alexander King, who has written a wonderful book called *Animal Dreaming: The Symbolic and Spiritual Language of Australasian Animals* (Rockpool, 2003), identifies the symbolism of snakes as transmutation. He goes on to say that just as a snake sheds its skin, it teaches us to discard all outgrown values and belief systems. 'Snake helps to harness qualities that promise to transmute us to higher levels, while simultaneously helping us to heal and rebirth.'

When I thought about this later, I realised that was what my cancer treatment was all about. I was shedding old skin and looking to heal and begin a new phase of life.

So did Percy pop in to bring me a message and perhaps some of nature's healing energy?

I like to think so.

13

Visions of Light

I had been warned to take care of my teeth and gums during the radiotherapy treatment, to rinse out my mouth before and after meals with bicarbonate of soda dissolved in water, and to use a soft toothbrush. It came as no surprise that one of my fillings suddenly decided to make a break for freedom, but I was fortunate to get an emergency dental appointment before heading back to Brisbane that week. This was a demonstration of the importance of heeding the very valuable advice given by the Brisbane Dental Hospital specialist in the lead up to radiotherapy.

Listening back to the audio diary I kept, I am still surprised at how well I was coping at this stage of the treatments. Apart from the rawness of my neck, I felt less stressed and calmer than I had been in previous weeks. At the time I put this down to the crystal-bed sessions that I had each weekend. I described them in my audio diary as a 'tremendous boon to have, to be able to relax, ask for healing and just accept it.' Thinking back, it was so beneficial that I could trust in the whole process and not let my fears get in the way.

That week, as I went into the next phase of my radio-therapy treatment, I added a new request to the protection I was creating before each tomo session. Up until that point I had been mentally creating a protective light around my teeth, jaws, saliva glands, lymph nodes and of course my vocal chords. This is a recommended practice for anyone exposing themselves to vulnerable situations with other people, and is an ideal practice for healers, nurses, counsellors and anyone dealing directly with the public. I know most psychics use this procedure to prevent energy drain when they are doing readings for people who are often stressed and emotional.

With my neck getting redder and more tender by the day, I began visualising a protective layer of light covering my skin across the throat area. My intention was to create protection that would allow the rays to do their work with minimal impact on the outer skin of my throat. With thirteen more appointments to go, I knew I had to do everything I could to make it easy on myself.

These techniques may seem a bit way out to many people but, believe me, they work — and if a previously sceptical broadcaster and journalist like me can accept this, then why not others?

I had also started to select a rune stone at the beginning of each week to get a message for the next group of treatments: as previously mentioned, each stone has a special message and I have always found the modern interpretations are akin to consulting my own inner wisdom. That week the message I received was 'trust', which I felt was most appropriate.

While I was in a state of deep meditation in one session, I unexpectedly connected with the spirit of my father who passed over in 1986. I had always felt sad that we had never been close during his lifetime. He was a quiet and very conservative man and I would have liked to know him better. Now the warmth of his unexpected contact was very comforting, even nurturing, and I suddenly felt closer to him than ever before. I knew he was there to give me support and comfort, and also felt certain that he was not preparing me to join him in the afterlife. He had already come through in a medium session with my friend Ezio DeAngelis, to be part of my book *No Goodbyes*, so I was not too surprised.

So now I was getting more and more support from both sides of the veil. Anne, who has natural healing abilities, was there each day with her cool hands to apply the prescribed cream to my neck and then put the dressings around an area that was by now very sensitive. Fortunately it was winter and I was able to button up a shirt to the collar so I didn't look like I had been in a motor accident. It's funny, but even at times like these I didn't want people staring at me. I just wanted to quietly go about my business and disappear into the background. That's something very different for someone who trained as an actor and then worked for years as a TV and radio presenter, enjoying the spotlight whenever it fell on me.

As the treatments mounted and my appetite dwindled, I was losing a little more weight each week, which pleased me. But the dietician was a little concerned and urged me to keep up the protein in my diet. I asked her whether this included more ice cream, and she laughingly agreed. Yeah, that's my kind of dietician.

I was feeling very pleased that even though the outside of my neck was becoming more and more red and raw, the throat area where the radiation was being directed was not causing any serious problems at all. With my taste buds being blasted five times a week, food had totally lost its appeal — that is except for ice cream and protein drinks. I had to make a conscious effort to eat three meals a day, and each serving was getting smaller and smaller. Anne did her best to come up with appetising dishes and we also found a couple of good takeaway places selling dishes that amazingly I could still taste. For someone who enjoys his food, this was a challenging time.

However, I did manage to find a way to enjoy a good meal. During each meditation on the tomo table I decided to visualise delicious meals enjoyed while in one of our very favourite cities in the world, Paris. *C'est si bon!* The dishes I visualised made my mouth water, but didn't help with the weight situation. Maybe I had discovered a new fad diet?

I felt grateful that my daughter Bec had reminded me of the powers of visualisation when I was preparing for my radiotherapy. It certainly helped me skim through each session, unlike some of the other patients, who I was told were finding it hard to cope with their daily treatments. I said a small prayer of thanks for being able to prepare myself and cope with the whole process the way I was doing.

I believe that everybody can come up with their own unique way of coping with cancer treatment if they are willing to give it a go. Where there is a will there's a way, my mother taught me as a child. So even though people may not always choose to follow my methods, taking responsibility for yourself and staying positive can open many doors.

14

A Very Long Weekend

As I write this on a Queen's Birthday holiday long weekend, my mind drifts back to what was happening on this exact holiday break during my treatment.

After a fairly uneventful week, Anne and I drove home looking forward to a three-day break from the hospital regimen. However, my body had other ideas. Waking on Saturday morning brought with it a lot of pain and discomfort. The night before my neck had more and more resembled a picture of extreme sunburn, and now it felt that way too. As a boy growing up in Bondi near the beach, it was customary to spend a lot of time enjoying the waves and playing outside in the extremely hot summer sun that is part of life in Australia.

Sun-worshipping was part of my life, often accompanied by blistering red skin as I turned my pale winter body into the tanned look we all desperately sought in those years. Waking up aching all over from sunburn was almost a rite of passage at the beginning of each summer. As I advanced in years, I realised the folly of this pursuit, especially as scientists discovered the 'hole in the ozone layer' that intensified the exposure to the sun's ultraviolet rays. Like many Australians,

I have paid for my youthful brown look with several skin cancers in recent years, including a melanoma on my shoulder which I was fortunate to have removed in its early stages.

So here I was, reliving the painful memories of my younger days, albeit in a very concentrated area of my body. During the previous week, as the discomfort increased, I had tried various creams, including a milk-based one that had recently hit the market, all to no avail. On that painful Saturday my local chemist suggested using aqueous cream, which offered only limited relief as the weekend dragged on painfully. So much for a welcome break. By the time we headed back to the hospital the following Tuesday for treatment number twenty-three, I was not looking forward to the remaining sessions. I didn't say as much to Anne, but I was becoming more and more concerned about how I would be able to cope from here on in, knowing that my neck would only become more and more raw.

However, those wonderful nurses in the oncology area told me that they would be able to help by applying a special dressing to my neck each day after the treatment. This involved applying the special sorboline cream they used in the oncology section, and then using a large padded dressing that wrapped right around my neck. I took a look in the mirror and it made me look like I had a broken neck. But at that stage I couldn't have cared less about my appearance, and it was winter and my shirt covered up half the dressing. Nobody even gave me a sideways glance in the next few weeks. Well, not that I observed anyway.

The main thing was that it helped me to cope with the pain and discomfort that had made the long weekend so miserable. The nurses gave me some dressings to be able to use at home on the weekends. Blessed relief. I was able to anticipate moving about quite freely and enjoying my time in Brisbane for those last couple of weeks.

15

My Very Own 'Night at the Opera'

I was now accustomed to each week at the hospital starting with a consultation with my oncologist, then a session with the dietician, followed by my first chat with Tomo for the week. After a quick check by Dr Charles, I got onto the scales to make sure I wasn't losing too much weight, and then it was off to the dietician to talk about how my diet was going, along with cheerful enquiries about the state of my bowels. The first time I was asked how my bowels were going, I irreverently replied, 'Fine thanks, how's yours?' That was met with a strange look. However the dieticians soon became accustomed to my bizarre sense of humour and we ended up having some humorous exchanges about all sorts of things — all related to diets, of course.

Anne usually came to the session with the dietician, as she was preparing my meals and wanted to make sure I was doing the right thing.

However, on this memorable day, the set order changed at the last minute and I was called into the treatment room before seeing the dietician. Afterwards, I proceeded to the nurse's station to have my dressing applied and was told to sit on a hospital bed as usual. The curtain was pulled around for privacy, creating a cosy little cubicle. My nurse decided to show one of the trainees how to apply my dressing, so all of a sudden I had two nurses fussing about my neck. Anne was allowed to sit in a visitor's chair next to the bed, so now there were four of us in my 'cubicle'.

Then I was asked if it would be all right if the dietician came in and had our chat while my dressing was being applied. 'No problem,' I replied. 'The more the merrier.' So there were five of us in my tiny nest. Cosy started to take on a new meaning.

As the trainee nurse was receiving instruction about applying the dressing, the dietician began to run down her checklist with me. While holding my head at certain angles, I was trying to divide my attention between enquiries about my dressing and pain level and chatting about my diet and capacity for eating ice creams. As the noise levels rose, the funny side of this appealed to me and I started cracking up with laughter. Laughter can be infectious, and the nurses saw the humour of the situation too and we enjoyed a mad moment or two. My dietician was not sure about all this, but a few moments later she too started laughing. The noise could not possibly go unnoticed and another nurse peered through the curtain to see what was causing the hilarity. Naturally she could not resist coming in for a moment to be part of what was by now resembling a tightly packed medical sardine can, the realisation of which brought on a new bout of laughter, mainly from me. Fortunately, there were no other patients around, so we did not disturb anyone.

Looking at the bunch of people around the bed, all seemingly speaking at once, my mind automatically went to that crazy scene in the Marx Brothers movie *A Night at the Opera* where all manner of people kept arriving and packing themselves into Groucho's tiny cabin on board a cruise ship. This has always been one of my favourite comic movie scenes and here I was living it for myself. (You can watch this hilarious scene on YouTube: 'A Night at the Opera Crowded Cabin Scene'.)

The hilarity only lasted a few minutes. But it made me remember that laughter can indeed be the best medicine. My neck seemed to hurt a lot less that day as I left the hospital.

16

Parting is Such Sweet Sorrow

Shakespeare's famous line from *Romeo and Juliet* seems most appropriate when I think back to the last days of my radiotherapy.

I had learned to cope with my 'neck burn' and to apply my own dressings, most of the time with Anne's expert help, so it became less of a problem than I had feared after the painful long weekend. The last couple of weeks of treatment cruised by with no dramas, each day much the same as the one before. So when the morning came for my thirty-fifth and final treatment, I looked around the tomotherapy treatment room for the last time and thanked the therapists who had been so supportive. They in turn informed me that I was one of their top patients, as I was always on time, had never caused a fuss and working with me was a breeze. This of course made me feel great, especially as they told me how so many patients arrive filled with fear and panic, and just settling them down before they could start a session was a major problem.

I mentioned how my meditation and visualisation techniques played such an important part in my mental and emotional preparation, and asked if it would help if I recorded a special meditation audio to help those having problems. But the radiotherapists seemed to think that most people would not take advantage of such help, for a variety of reasons, including being sceptical about such 'non-medical practices'. I found this a sad situation because so many people could be helped if only they would let go of their rigid beliefs about what is and isn't 'medical practice'. I know that embracing all manner of assistance and taking responsibility for my own healing made an enormous difference to my treatments and the subsequent healing time.

Such things as meditation, visualisation and an open, positive mindset are all now being embraced by many parts of the community, including the business sector. Corporate training programs are successfully embracing and integrating these and many more techniques to help their staff reduce stress and work more productively. Perhaps the medical fraternity needs to openly encourage people to explore some of these aids for themselves and not just stick to the old methods. I believe even introducing meditation would have widespread benefits for both staff and patients.

Anyway, for hospital or administrative staff working in this area, my offer remains on the table. I'll even omit my trips to Paris, opting for a more universal location, like a beautiful garden or a tropical island paradise.

Leaving Royal Brisbane Hospital with my battered old treatment card now completely filled, I felt mixed emotions as I walked to where my car was parked. Of course I was glad to be getting back to my *normal* life, but strangely the regimen that I had adopted for nearly two months had become more than just habit. It was so easy to escape from the daily routine I was used to and embrace a different lifestyle, even for just a few weeks. Thinking about the last seven weeks, I wondered how easy it would be to get back home and resume my normal life. My voice was very scratchy at this point, with a dry mouth and throat, and I was not comfortable doing a lot of talking, preferring instead to rest my voice — a radical departure for a long-time broadcaster. But it probably suited Anne as she could keep me in line and not get much back chat.

There were a couple of concerns that niggled away in the back of my mind over the last few days of radiotherapy. My voice was the main concern. I wondered whether I would be able to do any more freelance voice work. My pre-recorded radio programs on RadioOutThere.com would run out, so would my voice be strong enough and sound clear enough to start interviewing again? Although only a weekly program, its structure is based around interviewing people from all around the world and I had no desire to give it up. I decided that if I was meant to keep working on radio and doing voiceovers, then my voice would recover accordingly. If not? Well, I had enjoyed a long run — just on fifty years as a radio and TV presenter — and I consoled myself with the thought that there was always my writing to keep my mind active. I would get my voice out there somehow.

All these thoughts flashed through my mind the last time I made the ten-minute drive back to the apartment at Spring Hill to collect Anne and head back home. I was grateful that despite the discomfort of my neck I was still able to drive to and from the hospital each day without any problems.

As a parting message Dr Charles told me to protect my neck and throat from the sun while I was healing, and to make sure I wore a hat. We called into a shopping complex on the way home to buy a scarf to wrap around my throat. This proved a bit of a task as the sunny climes of Queensland and northern New South Wales do not lend themselves to men's scarves, especially soft ones for guys with raw red necks. I eventually succeeded in tracking a couple down and arrived home looking like I was heading off to the snow country. I also managed to find a large white floppy hat for extra shade. I looked quite a sight, especially when I teamed them all up with dark glasses. Now when I went for a walk I *was* getting some sideways glances.

About six weeks later my energy returned sufficiently for me to try a mid-week game of social tennis. Off I trotted with my floppy hat and flowing scarf to see if I could muster enough strength to hit a tennis ball. The other members of the group took pity on me and I played with three women for my big return. Despite my big white hat falling off whenever I lurched towards the ball, I managed to stagger through a set before collapsing into a chair. I still can't remember whether my partner and I even won a single game, but at least I had made the effort. It took a few more weeks before I could play reasonably decent tennis again, and then only for two eight-game social sets with a big rest break in between. But each week I was feeling stronger and more confident about my new life, hopefully now free from cancer.

Slowly, slowly, I started back recording radio programs, drinking loads of water to keep my throat lubricated. I even recorded a couple of small voiceovers, thankful that I wasn't being asked to do a complicated commercial read or a large narration. Maybe my agent was protecting me, just making sure I didn't take on too much. The more I did, the more I discovered that Dr Charles had indeed been able to avoid frying my vocal chords and lymph nodes.

Of course I continued having crystal-bed treatments and doing my meditation. My friend Glenda Anderson also gave me a couple of healing sessions to clear the negative energy that had accumulated in my system. As the first couple of weeks passed after my final treatment, I tuned in to my intuition and felt quietly confident that the radiotherapy had done its job.

Nevertheless, that little voice that niggled in my thoughts was having a field day as I drove back to the hospital several weeks later to hear the final verdict. *Would I get the all-clear as my intuition told me, or were those thirty-five visits to Tomo in vain?* The feeling of jangling nerves increased the closer I got to the hospital. The fact that I still had to undergo one more PET scan to verify the success or otherwise of the radiotherapy played on my mind.

After the scan the nursing staff provide you with a sandwich and a cup of tea, and as I sat munching my tasteless lunch my mind was still swirling with thoughts of what might or might not be. A couple of hours' wait was worth it all when I got the initial all-clear from the oncologist, and all remaining doubts were lifted from my mind.

Sure, it was very early days, but I knew I was well on the road to healing.

17

The Year After

It is now over three years since my treatments finished.

The first year was a time of healing slowly, taking things one day at a time. I gradually regained the energy that had disappeared so easily, and finally achieved the peace of mind that seemed so far away at the time of diagnosis. It took a full twelve months to do a full day's work again without having to sit down and rest after any kind of exertion. I can even manage a short burst of gardening with no dizzy spells and breathlessness. It took twelve months for my salivary glands to get back to almost-full production and I didn't need to constantly chew gum to avoid dry mouth syndrome. It took some eight months for my taste buds to really start working again, so I could enjoy a very mild curry and even have a glass of wine that didn't taste like vinegar. By the end of the year I was also able to play two or three sets of tennis without needing a rest in between each set. Mind you, hitting the ball consistently and well was a completely different question.

My initial concern about my vocal chords being badly affected by the radiotherapy proved to be a false alarm. With my careful personal preparation and the highly focused technology of the tomo machine, my vocal abilities have emerged relatively unscathed. My voice is still a little croaky from time to time, especially first thing in the morning, but I am still able to work as a radio presenter and voice artist, with an ever-present glass of water by my side.

Six weeks after my treatments finished, my book *Afterlife: Uncovering the Secrets of Life After Death* was published in America. This meant I was required to do a round of publicity interviews to help promote the book. I was delightfully surprised to be invited to appear on the iconic radio show 'Coast to Coast', which is broadcast to North America and beyond, and somewhat stunned to discover the interview would last for three hours. If ever my voice was going to be tested, this was it. It went off without a hitch and I received a load of positive audience feedback, so I must have sounded okay. This was followed by several more interviews on other programs, lasting up to an hour each, so the old vocal chords really came up trumps.

One practice which I believe contributed to my recovery is known as oil pulling. This is an ancient Ayurvedic practice that involves swishing oil around the mouth for fifteen to twenty minutes first thing in the morning to kill harmful oral bacteria. Oil pulling is a popular folk remedy in India and it became known in the west when Dr Fedor Karach presented a paper on it to a Ukrainian medical conference in the early 1990s, claiming it was also a traditional Russian practice. Today entire books have been written about oil pulling and the online health world buzzes with testimonies regarding its apparent health benefits. Starting each morning with fifteen minutes of oil pulling using organic coconut oil, I believe has helped my throat greatly during and after my radiotherapy. Even my dentist fully endorsed the practice.

The main problem that lingered, however, was an outbreak of eczema or dermatitis which started during my treatment and got steadily worse over the next few months. It cleared for a while but returned with a vengeance six months down the track at the beginning of the new year. I can only put it down to the stress that my body was not able to release after my treatments finished. But my doctor maintained that, although the connection is possible, it is not a common occurrence. As I am a great proponent of the correlation between emotions and physical illness, I decided to investigate it further.

The American author Louise Hay, a noted expert in this field, suggests that eczema involves 'mental disruptions'. In her book *The Body is the Barometer of the Soul*, Annette Noontil relates dermatitis to 'stirred up emotions of being unworthy or inadequate'. These emotional triggers struck a chord with me and I set about working on the problem with meditation techniques and a change of lifestyle. My friend Judith Richards also helped me with hypnotherapy techniques to ease the problem.

Twelve months after the radiotherapy treatments, I was suffering badly from this very intrusive and painful skin condition. However, I received a very valuable birthday present after putting out a cry for help to the universe. Anne and I went for a drive on my birthday to explore the lovely coastline near where I live. We stopped for lunch at a coastal resort and, with my taste buds working nicely, enjoyed a Thai meal. After lunch we went for a walk to explore the town and just 'happened' on a clinic that specialises in skin problems. We went inside and spoke to the owner, who had conveniently just dropped in for a few minutes on his day off but offered to give me a test. As he initially suspected, I had all the symptoms of candida, and he prescribed a treatment program for me. The situation confirmed my belief that some things are just 'meant to be' — it was no coincidence that he was in the clinic for a few minutes when we stumbled upon it after lunch. I thanked the powers that set up the whole scenario, figuring that my guardian angel had come up with a unique birthday gift.

After being diagnosed with candida as the trigger for this very disturbing skin condition, I went on a strict gluten-free diet. I avoided wheat and other grains, and also went on a sugar-elimination and dairy-free diet, which soon payed dividends. After four months of gluten-, dairy- and sugar-free food, I managed to rid my body of the candida parasite that had attached itself to me. Sadly that also meant the end of my ice cream diet. But things were beginning to look up, and I could definitely see a light at the end of the tunnel.

Another big plus was the kilos that dropped away when I gave up sugar and sugar-related products such as desserts, breakfast cereals, sauces, jams and snacks. I had already shed around ten kilos during my radiotherapy treatments and now, with sugar off the menu, I dropped another four kilos in less than three weeks. I tried to explain this to a friend whose weight has ballooned and he blithely informed me that he only uses one teaspoon of sugar in his tea and coffee. Like most people, he didn't realise how much sugar there is in the majority of products on supermarket shelves.

My energy levels also fluctuated, often daily. One morning I would wake full of beans and the next day I could hardly drag one foot after another. This despite the fact I was taking it easy during the day and getting plenty of rest at night. The doctors all told me that I had to be patient because I was returning physically and emotionally to what I would regard as normal. As one doctor explained, radiation kills the bad cells, but it targets the good cells as well and it takes time for them to regenerate.

But for those of us who go through the rigours of cancer with its challenging and harrowing times, is there such a thing as 'returning to normal'? If so, can we define what is normal and what is not? Those are tough questions at the best of times.

Just as I thought I was in the clear and as my skin was getting healthier every day, my left ankle became infected and the whole calf and foot ballooned, making it difficult and painful to walk. Once again I combined mainstream and complementary treatments, as my alternative therapist told me that sometimes medications such as antibiotics are not the best course of action. Unfortunately, scans revealed what is known as 'incompetent veins' in my left leg and I have to wear a compression stocking to keep the blood flowing evenly. Another operation loomed large on the horizon to solve this problem. More damned hospitals.

Was this a residual effect of my cancer treatment or just my body getting older, as my doctor suggested? Does it really matter in the long run?

I eventually did have the operation and had the recalcitrant veins removed, which made life a lot easier, even if it did mean another bout of surgery.

I guess a lot of people who recover from cancer are just thankful that they can get on with their lives, but the whole event made me stop and think. I believe that everything in life happens for a reason, and having an extreme health condition certainly made me reflect on why it all happened. I once read that we all either create, attract or accept everything in our life, and after analysing it I understood the concept entirely. So what was the reason my body *created* this cancerous growth in my throat? Or did I *attract* it for some reason? I certainly did not *accept* it and so decided to rid myself of the disease. Maybe my cancer could be explained medically, but what about the deeper meaning of what happened? What lessons has it brought, and what changes?

Of course, it is all too easy to blithely say that having cancer has made me look at my life and express gratitude for still being alive. That is a given coming through any life-threatening situation. Naturally, I am grateful that my cancer was diagnosed at an early stage, and after three years the signs are all positive that it has been eliminated from my system. However, at the time of writing, there are still two years remaining before the doctors give the final all clear, so for me the question is, *what have I learned from the experience and what do I have to do to stay healthy?*

Researching my two books on the afterlife showed me that although most of our life events are determined by free will, there are certain destiny points that we face at various times. Many people use the phrase 'it was meant to be', and for me this is just another way of labelling a destiny point that impacted them in some way. It is how we react to these destiny points that form the next phase of our lives.

I was not prepared to shrug it all off, forget about the past and just get on with life without another thought, so I started to do some inner reflection to get more answers. Answers that would help me understand why I had to go through this painful and stress-laden time, and to make sure that I would benefit from the knowledge.

The first thing that came to mind was to stop being so hard on myself when I make a mistake. If, like a lot of people, I do something stupid or clumsy, I tend to berate myself: *for heaven's sake, Barry, what's the matter with you, stop being stupid* has been a typical frustrated reaction that I have expressed out loud all too often.

We all make mistakes. It's the best way of learning what not to do next time. The trick is not to keep repeating the same mistakes. That *is* being stupid.

Okay, so that is lesson number one.

The importance of family was another big wake-up call for me. It is so easy to take our loved ones for granted and be totally immersed in our own personal little world at the expense of family and friends. The strength and support that my close family in particular gave me during my cancer treatment helped me to cope with one of the most difficult periods of my life. The love and encouragement that Anne gave me has deepened and strengthened the bonds of our relationship. I probably would have physically survived if I had had to do it on my own, but I'm not sure how I would have got through it emotionally. My family's love and support during my ordeal is something that will stay with me forever and has helped me grow as a person.

Another big lesson was to think about what I want to achieve in my life — for however many years I have left. We tend to look back each New Year's Eve, surprised at how quickly the months have sped by, wondering what we managed to achieve and vowing to do things differently in the next year.

Having undergone the rigours of cancer was the same as reviewing the past and looking to the future. I determined to work out my priorities, stop worrying about what *might* happen and find the best balance between work, family and personal growth that I can. I also started a bucket list of all the places I would like to visit with Anne before we are too old, or too broke, to travel. (This list alone will keep a travel agent busy for quite some time.)

Finally I now accept that the subconscious belief that I deserved to die, which I discovered in my hypnotherapy session, has been put to rest. I now believe that I deserve to fully live, love and be happy for whatever remains of my natural life.

After receiving the all clear, I also wished to express my thanks to the medical staff at Royal Brisbane Hospital and the support team at Cancer NSW. I wondered how best to get the word out about these wonderful people. The answer came in the weeks and months following my radiotherapy program, when so many people I shared my experiences with told me that I had to write a book about it. I realised that this book could also give hope to, and motivate, those who have to face the crisis of cancer — whether it be for their own journey or for someone they love.

I have come to accept that my experience was not only part of my destiny in this lifetime but something that has helped me grow as a person. For this I am truly grateful.

However, I must emphasise that this is *my experience*. I am not telling people what to do or how to go about their own treatment program. The techniques I used and the help and support I received make up my unique experience. Everybody has their own journey — in life no two stories are the same.

18

Looking within for Answers

As I looked back on this period of great turmoil in my life, I decided to explore my inner wisdom by consulting the rune stones one more time.

Asking what caused my cancer, I drew the Rune of Disruption, which was hardly surprising. The text described this as 'the Great Awakener, of elemental disruption, of events totally beyond your control'. It went on to say that 'there is nothing trivial about this Rune, and the more severe the disruption, the more it signified the timely requirements for your growth'. The message concluded by saying that the universe and my own soul were demanding that I did indeed grow as a person.

The accuracy of the message took my breath away. As an astrologer, I know that a key 'trigger planet' for sudden and life-changing events in my life is Uranus, acknowledged as, you guessed it, 'the Great Awakener'.

I posed the question to myself: *What did I need to learn from the experience?* I then drew the Rune of Separation, which was upside down, or reversed. The message here was that it is important not to be 'bound by old conditioning' and I need 'to let my life flow, and not be rigid and stuck in the past.' The message concluded, 'remember, we do without doing, and everything gets done.'

When I analysed the message, I realised that by drawing this rune my intuition was simply telling me to release the past and trust that the future will take care of itself. In other words, let go, stop worrying and trust that everything in my life is now on track — it is vital to move on and not simply go back to the habits and limitations of my old lifestyle. The past is the past and must be accepted as such. For me, an important part of my new direction was a radical change of diet. Sugar-laden and other unhealthy supermarket foods have given way to fresh, locally grown products, organic where possible. I decided to go dairy and gluten free, and my daily wine or two with dinner is now reduced to an occasional glass of red wine. I know I need to respect my body and be aware of the fuel I put into it. Mind you, being human, I do have an occasional breakout.

This second message summarised the whole cancer experience for me.

A few days later I received a real surprise. It was almost as if I had to wait for this information until I was ready to receive it.

Sorting through some personal papers, I came upon my father's death certificate dated May 1986. I was working in radio in Vienna when he passed and my brother Mike had registered the details. As my eyes drifted down the page, I came to cause of death, and got such a jolt that I almost dropped the certificate.

Cause number one was 'squamous cell carcinoma of the lung'. I knew my father had passed from lung cancer but this was the first time that squamous cell carcinoma, or SCC, meant something in my life.

My thoughts flashed back to that obnoxious doctor who blithely informed me that my squamous cell carcinoma was triggered by HPV. Now I discovered that my father had an SCC in his lung. I don't believe in *coincidences* of this nature, so could it be that my cancer at the base of my throat was genetically influenced? My local doctor thinks otherwise but, according to some research, in rare cases inherited genes can influence cancer. And 50 per cent of our DNA comes from one parent and the other half from the other parent.

My mind raced with possibilities. My father fought in World War II and, like most soldiers, was a heavy smoker before quitting in his mid to late forties. He was diagnosed with lung cancer in his sixties. My throat cancer was discovered just after I turned seventy. Although I have never smoked, I made regular appearances as an MC for a cigarette company for many years, spending hours in rooms filled with the haze of tobacco smoke and mixing with heavy smokers. Various family members and my two ex-wives smoked regularly around me, and my late partner Judy was a heavy smoker when we met (I was delighted to be able to help her give that filthy habit away before she passed).

I woke one morning with another thought swirling in my mind. I recalled the growing effect that being in the presence of smokers has had on me for the last fifteen years. In the time leading up to the diagnosis of cancer, a mere whiff of cigarette smoke was enough to turn my stomach. I consciously avoided people who were smoking, whether it was in the street or at a social function. This is not a coincidence in my mind. It was my body giving me a very clear message: *cigarette smoke is poison for your system.*

Now, more than two years after my cancer treatments concluded, I do not have the same extreme reaction, but I do escape cigarette smoke as fast as I can.

There is still a lot of controversy over the effects of passive smoking, but once again my research turned up some significant information. I discovered a relevant piece of information on the website of the American Cancer Society (www.cancer.org/cancer/cancercauses/tobaccocancer/second hand-smoke):

> Secondhand smoke (SHS) is also called environmental tobacco smoke (ETS) … Non-smokers who breathe in SHS take in nicotine and toxic chemicals in the same way smokers do. The more SHS you breathe, the higher the levels of these harmful chemicals in your body.
>
> Secondhand smoke is known to cause cancer. It has more than 7,000 chemicals, including at least 70 that can cause cancer.
>
> …
>
> SHS causes lung cancer. There's also some evidence suggesting it might be linked in adults to cancers of the:
>
> Larynx (voice box)
> Pharynx (throat)
> Nasal sinuses
> Brain
> Bladder
> Rectum
> Stomach
> Breast

It's possibly linked in children to:

Lymphoma
Leukemia
Liver cancers
Brain tumors

I feel that at last I have found important answers to questions that had been troubling me since the original diagnosis, which did not resonate with my gut instinct.

And one thing I have proven is that I have developed very high intuitive abilities in the last twenty-five years.

19

The Changes to My Life

As I put the final touches to this story more than three years after my treatment, I know deep down that I have changed considerably. Things that used to upset and worry me no longer have the same disturbing effects. I have become more philosophical about life in general, and my life in particular. That's not to say I still don't experience stressful situations or get upset, but I am consciously doing my best to accept and move on whenever possible.

No longer do I have the feeling of having to prove myself and my beliefs to people who previously challenged what I stand for, nor do I have the same drive to put in a full day's work — unless I feel like it. Stress factors such as deadlines and keeping the bank manager happy do not have the same importance as in the past. I am happy to sit on my deck in the sunshine, sipping a cup of tea and admiring my splendid mountain outlook, surrounded by the sounds of nature. Some might refer to this as meditation. I prefer to think of it as quiet time when I can separate my mind from the hurly-burly of everyday life. If and when I feel inclined, I wander into my office and do some writing or record an interview for my radio program. If freelance work opportunities like voiceovers or speaking engagements present themselves from time to time, I am happy to embrace them, but not with the same compulsive need that drove me in the past. Whether the pace will pick up in the near future will be my decision.

As for the thought of my cancer returning, or perhaps taking another form which might end up being fatal, I do not even give it a passing thought. Having written extensively about the afterlife, I have absolutely no fear of death. Instead I am more interested in bringing my life into balance. This includes a great sense of gratitude for being given this opportunity to come to these realisations, and also for the knowledge of the importance of love in my life.

Love for my family and friends, and most importantly a deeper love for my partner Anne who has played such a vital part in my journey through cancer and beyond.

Now it's over to Anne for her side of the story.

PART II

Travelling with Cancer: A Companion's Journey

by Anne Morjanoff

1

The Road Ahead

Summer. Thirty-six degrees centigrade — and the early morning temperature was *still* rising. Sweltering, mind-numbing conditions. Preparing for departure was befuddling. In the dense clammy humidity we groped for adequate clothing, anticipating that whatever was chosen would soon be damp and clinging uncomfortably. But we persevered. Despite the weather, there was a commitment.

By 11 am a heat haze obscured the sky and the gauge had advanced to above 40 degrees centigrade. At 3.15 pm the searing heat reached a record-breaking 46 degrees. 18 January 2013 was a significant day for many reasons, most of which were yet to reveal themselves. Barry and I were unaware of the fast-forward effect about to transform the peaks and valleys of our lives.

Finally we were in the car and driving through the sultry northern suburbs of Sydney to join the F3 Freeway. Travelling three hours to a family funeral in muggy heat felt like an endurance test, despite air-conditioning in the car. We listened uneasily to state-wide warnings on the radio about heavy traffic congestion and significant delays because of motor accidents in the extremely torrid conditions. Services on almost every rail network were affected. The overloaded electricity grid struggled with supply issues, affected by damaged overhead and overheated power lines. Sombre announcements included advice to take appropriate measures to avoid heat stroke and to carry water to keep hydrated. Adventurous campers were sensibly advised to shelter and stay out of harm's way. Bushfire notifications and warnings of sizzling conditions were broadcast. Residents were directed to be vigilant and to be on the lookout for snakes trying to seek refuge in cool places, even in homes: apparently reptiles prefer to hide under cover at about 30 degrees centigrade — any hotter could kill them. (The Chinese year of the snake was about to commence on 4 February. The snake *element* is said to be mainly fire, so including them in contingency plans was understandably important.)

The summer of 2013 produced an unprecedented heatwave in terms of duration and intensity, breaking the previous Australian weather record set in 1939. The Chinese astrology prediction was that 2013 would generally be a mix of good and bad fortune. We certainly hadn't expected the year ahead to be as unpredictable as it turned out to be.

At 11.30 am we arrived at our destination in East Maitland, and joined a large crowd at St Peter's Church. The clergy gained our great admiration for being fully robed, even wearing white stoles in honour of the deceased: Barry's cousin Russell had been a stickler for 'proper attire', whatever the circumstances. A moving tribute by Russell's daughter Kate was deeply heartfelt. Her eulogy was engrossing, and sometimes entertaining, so we could almost ignore the stifling heat. Occasionally the 'order of service' was used to wave a wisp of air across a perspiring face. Someone had provided an electric fan in an attempt to cool the choir, although I'm not sure that it was effective judging by their glistening red faces. However, they managed to sing on enthusiastically with our blessing.

After farewelling the coffin and procession of clergy, we adjourned for refreshments provided at the wake next door. We gulped cooling drinks while catching up with Barry's extended family. Around mid-afternoon we reluctantly left them for the three-hour drive back to Sydney. The temperature had soared to its record-breaking maximum. Meteorologists were forecasting fearsome weather changes, with wild thunderstorms expected to bring a rapid drop in temperature.

A funeral sometimes results in introspection about our own mortality. Throughout that irksome journey, we discussed our feelings about life and death. We shared experiences, sorrowful personal losses and our mundane philosophies on death and dying, not expecting it to be any more than a normal reaction to the passing of a family member.

Normally we'd skirt around such discussions. But maybe as we are getting older we need to open the door just a little to peek at the subject. If there were a choice, would we want to stay at home or go to an aged-care facility? Each of us had different needs that would have to be taken into account. Quietly we agreed to be practical when the time came. Delaying the discussion would likely add strain to family members if practicalities hadn't been discussed and resolved, potentially leaving them struggling to make decisions on our behalf in difficult circumstances. There was also the possibility of conflict among them about how to navigate that last journey. It was most important, we decided, to focus on living well and passing with dignity.

Half an hour from home we abruptly drove into the precipitous though predicted 'clearing storm' of ferocious blinding rain, fierce winds and flying branches. We slowed in low visibility, then halted behind a police car and sodden policemen blocking our way. Hunched against the storm's force, they hauled away broken branches strewn across the roadway. We watched anxiously as they battled to clear a large branch and other debris, with leaves, twigs and small branches flying all about them. Eventually, they waved us forward and we continued our journey, keeping a sharp lookout for any further hazards. (A few weeks later I happened to pull up alongside the same police car at a service station, and asked the young driver if he was one of those who had cleared the way for us. 'Yes,' he acknowledged. I was pleased to offer sincere thanks for his efforts. 'All in a day's work,' he replied with a grin. They saved us that day and I'm still very grateful. Thanks guys.)

By the time we arrived home, the savage storm had exhausted itself but we couldn't settle. The temperature was down to 30 degrees centigrade. At dusk we took refuge in our local beach pool — just melting into it, bliss — until the southerly buster wind sprang up. It was so strong we joked about being blown all the way to New Zealand. Fleeing home we consoled ourselves by dipping into creamy crunchy mango with macadamia ice cream — so soothing and temptingly delicious we could barely control impulsive spoon-dipping into the tub.

What a turbulent and curious day. What a bizarre weather event to start a *very* bewildering year.

It touches on my own conviction that DIVINE WISDOM can speak, in a penetrating call, to *all human beings*, in one way or another, offering an assurance that life is not just like a leaf, flown here and there by the wind, but it *is* a challenge — expecting an honest response.

— Revd Peter Baron

Barry had arrived to stay with me in Sydney from his home in northern New South Wales the day before the funeral. Coughing frequently, or trying to subdue a cough, he was spluttering his way through conversations far more than usual. His constant throat clearing and coughing had caused me considerable concern over the years since meeting him nearly thirteen years earlier in the year 2000. From time to time I had suggested he get medical advice about it, mostly eliciting a defensive response that he was fine. Barry firmly asserted that he had consulted a medical practitioner some time ago and had passed the tests with flying colours, so he was fine. Resolutely and definitely — if not defiantly — fine. But this time was somehow different. His normal dulcet announcer's voice was crackling and coarse. His coughing was severely pronounced and he said it felt like something was constantly stuck in his throat. Seeing him cough up a few specks of blood jarred us both. Rather forcefully, I urged him yet again to get medical advice. This time he promised to visit his doctor when he returned home at the end of the month.

Finally he's going to consult a professional. What a relief. Over the years it's been difficult to convince Barry to take any course of action unless he wants to and it agrees with his sense of timing. An insightful friend of ours had once nicknamed him the Time Lord because he's always such a stickler for time. An apt description, especially when added to his personal motto, 'I did it my way.'

Barry returned to his home over 800 kilometres away at the end of January. Apparently he expected 2013 to be a fairly routine year.

I started pondering the effects of putting things off. Since we normally don't know when our time is up, how would we feel to discover that our prospects were prematurely limited? It seems to me that when we reflect, make a choice and become decisive, it's timely to start living with dedicated awareness. Then we can really appreciate who we are and who we are travelling with each day.

2

Referral

Barry would normally call at least once a day by phone or he'd Skype. He kept me up to date when finally he went to see his local doctor about his constant coughing. Thank goodness the doctor immediately referred him to Dr Tim, an ear, nose and throat specialist. They seemed to develop a good rapport right from the start, although Barry's daily updates left me feeling faintly uneasy. There seemed to be gaps in the information he passed on and I couldn't quite grasp the bigger picture and possible implications. This was unchartered territory, and worrisome, and I had constant doubts about the best way to deal with it all.

Dr Tim referred Barry for a series of investigatory scans and tests. I found his feedback was a bit scary because we were suddenly swept up in medical procedures that we were totally unfamiliar with and which we hadn't been prepared for — even though Barry treated it all rather matter of factly. I asked many insistent questions, which revealed my lack of knowledge and I found myself feeling 'out of the loop' because he couldn't answer satisfactorily. He went along with the appointments and processes, sometimes in a dim haze it seemed to me, without being aware of where this road was taking him or what he would encounter along the way. At this stage, we were barely managing to cope with how things were unfolding, let alone being able to predict what would happen if things got worse.

I really felt the impact of the 800 kilometres between us, especially when it became obvious that surgery was required. *What were they thinking to be picking up a scalpel so quickly —* *had they done sufficient research?* I asked myself.

Many scenarios fluttered in and out of my mind, raising questions which mostly remained unanswered, and leaving us hovering in the midst of uncertainty. I saw the biggest hurdle being ignorance, bringing up a clutch of despairing 'what ifs'. Subtle fears hovered. It seemed everyone knew someone with symptoms corresponding to Barry's and many diverse opinions were offered about the best approaches to treatment. In an effort to be informed, we poured over literature. Some of the material proved worthwhile, some we ignored or rejected, some provided a flash of insight. Who were we to trust? What information is reliable, proven and trustworthy? Too much conflicting information muddles the head, and emotions gather in knots of uneasiness — inner turmoil reigns. That's when Barry's composure faltered. His 'normal' world had been turned upside down. His 'normal' reliable life landmarks were indistinct. Fear stalked him and worry creeped up, snapping on his heels.

Stumbling through emotional tangles, Barry landed somewhere in the middle of overwhelmed. As if asleep, submerged in myriad tremors, he needed to withdraw attention from the negative thoughts that were feeding them. As much as we discussed varying opinions and options, a little time out was necessary to get it all into perspective. At this point, his meditation practices became indispensable. He took himself off to consult his inner knowing.

Fear can hit us all at times and, when added to other associated emotions, it can be quite gut-wrenching. And reactions are very personal. What one person finds tolerable is not so for another. Confronting the issues can lead to unearthing amazing courage in the face of unknown outcomes. Barry was not going to back off from this challenge.

The fear of painful physical suffering can be debilitating unless faced. So he set about addressing and attempting to release the fear, with its emotional tugs and paralysing tensions, endeavouring to avoid being dominated by them. After some time, when chaos abated and conflicts no longer held sway, a calmer attitude emerged. He embraced an opportunity for transformation and, with the situation seeming less scary, discovered a more balanced approach to whatever lay ahead. He developed an aptitude to cope with the situation and to move past the constrictions. He appeared to be more confident of his own abilities in preparing for the challenges ahead. It was as if his mind was re-set, to see past outmoded methods of approaching obstacles.

Within two weeks of Barry's return to his home, I flew up to join him on his unpredictable journey.

In the meantime, he had continued with all the usual activities associated with his internet radio program and voice recording work. He conducted interviews, read and reviewed books, met up with his friends and colleagues and played tennis. He was not ready to make any changes to his normal lifestyle. So I followed suit. Business as usual.

For the next phase, re-organising my circumstances in Sydney became a priority before joining Barry. My family were very concerned and supportive. His family were all within a two-hour drive of his home. What a blessing that they were so close to him at this time.

Barry had sold his house in Sydney in 2010 — a three-minute drive from my home — and moved north to be closer to family, friends and an interesting new project. After a pilgrimage to Brazil, he had begun talking about making a new life away from the hustle and bustle of Sydney and had decided to put his house on the market. It was a difficult time for me since my father had recently passed away. My close friends were especially considerate, seeing me through my bereavement with numerous coffee mornings and putting up with my cheerless face and forlorn mutterings. I needed to stay put in Sydney, close to the support group of my family and friends — it was hugely important for me to be within easy visiting range of them all. I was grateful for their companionship and sustenance, and ultimately felt as if the light was emerging from behind a dark cloud bank as I started to appreciate a new sense of community. Opening to a renewed sense of purpose was still a little way off.

When his house sold, Barry decided that we would commute to see each other. It was not always easy, and sometimes disruptive, but workable. And it was not my choice, but Barry was keen to take part with his mates on a project that had taken his interest. So off he went. His new life unfolded fairly uneventfully, although not according to plan. The schemes hatched in Brazil had seemed feasible from a distance, but when tested on home soil had failed to eventuate.

We adjusted to the new life circumstances. Barry did make a point of including me in his new home renovations, which appealed to me. It was very pleasing to see the house's tired, gloomy interior transformed into a lighter and more attractive space. (His builder was especially diligent, and even now the energy he put into the renovation is palpable.) Barry wrote another book and was thankful for the quiet country surroundings. He asked me to help edit his writings, which I did, mostly from afar.

In 2013, three years after leaving Sydney and being confronted with health problems, our priorities changed. We planned to address issues one step at a time and see how things progressed. We would tackle each phase as it occurred. Maybe this way we could circumvent worries about what might or might not happen in the future. The moment of 'now' would indicate the way forward. Being together was an important part of the process, drawing on our combined strength and determination to face whatever lay ahead.

It was also helpful when caring callers asked about Barry's health and got past his standard response of 'fine, thanks'. Some people respected where he was at, yet still wanted to know and understand the difficulties he was experiencing. It was good to see his relief at not being alone on this journey and recognising the genuine connection and concern when friends suggested he 'call anytime, whatever the reason'. He welcomed and appreciated their support.

With the decision made to head north, I swung into action. Changes of plan don't always happen at the most convenient times. My daughter had just moved house and was in the midst of unpacking and organising her new home in preparation for my grandson to begin secondary school, so there was a lot happening and more than a little upheaval and adjustment required. Workmen's quotes for essential house repairs were piling up at my place, and I had just enough time for some urgent electrical work before departing.

Who knew what was ahead. There were changes afoot for sure.

When you spend time worrying,
You're simply using your imagination
To create things you don't want.
— Anonymous

3

Ultrasound

Barry and I made our way to the hospital, where he filled in the obligatory forms at the reception desk. Large muted television screens on the waiting-room walls provided a momentary diversion from the reason of our visit. The displaced images seemed so out of place with what we were experiencing. The receptionist answered a phone enquiry efficiently and quietly. Someone emerged from behind a panel to chat with her. We tensed with apprehension and the inactivity of waiting.

We were used to being gainfully occupied, Barry with interviews, radio programs and writing, and me focused on family, home, casual work and assisting with his writing or editing. I also did volunteer mentoring for LifeCircle, a Sydney-based organisation which provides support for home-based carers of the terminally ill and encourages people to make informed decisions about advance care planning and other issues. Would it become necessary to draw on these resources myself — a worrisome thought.

Finally a slight young man took us through stark corridors towards the radiation rooms. I was curious to see where the ultrasound would be carried out. Staff members pointed out the equipment in a small, confined, windowless room, lit only by an overhead light. There was a lot of stainless steel — it was certainly not very homely. Barry made innocuous comments, which brought smiles to their faces. He was in good form and was expecting to pass this test with flying colours. Attendants handed me his possessions and asked me to wait in the corridor outside, away from exposure to the radiation.

Sitting in isolation, I was engulfed by anxiety. My breathing felt restricted and I became uncomfortably warm. Alone with my thoughts, I suddenly had a flashback to similar hospital surroundings when my mother had been taken seriously ill many years ago. It was the time of the Eastern Seaboard Fires in January 1994 and I'd driven almost two hours to visit her in a regional hospital. The whole of Sydney was on alert, ringed by raging bushfires. Ash showered over the suburbs, igniting spot fires. Helicopters water-bombed inaccessible roaring blazes. Flames gusted furiously through treetops against orange skies. Many routes heading north out of Sydney were obscured by whirling dense smoke. I was lucky to get through before the roads were closed.

My mother was severely agitated when I arrived, and begged me to get her transferred to the care of her specialist in the city or she would certainly die. I tried in vain to calm her and she only became quiet once I'd promised that she'd be moved. Her instincts were ominously accurate, and even though I had her hastily transferred to the care of her trusted consultant in Sydney, it was too late. My mother had already become infected in hospital with the dreaded golden staph bacteria. She had entered the regional hospital with a conventional urinary tract infection and left with a death sentence at the age of only sixty-nine. Two young Sydney doctors confirmed her intuition a short time later, saying there was nothing they could do and she would die soon. Distressed, I sat scrutinising their blank faces, searching for some sign of hope. I was barely able to comprehend their verdict, delivered impassively, without any semblance of a sympathetic bedside manner. My life was about to become extremely challenging.

Emerging from my disturbing reverie, I realised it was not a good time to dwell on unsettling and intrusive memories. My mother had passed away almost twenty years earlier and it was time to return to the present. I needed to focus on Barry having a positive outcome. It was time to be practical. Gripping his possessions tightly, I bundled them neatly and waited patiently. Background humming took my attention. Was that Barry's machine at work? Footsteps approached, hospital personnel appeared and then disappeared into a nearby passage. I waited.

Time dissolved into empty space. My reverie was quietly interrupted and I was invited to join Barry to see the ultrasound images of his throat. He was sitting up, tidying his gown and couldn't see the screen. Standing behind the technician, I watched as he intently scanned, re-scanned, measured and filed a number of images. Something resembling a cauliflower was intriguing him. The measuring device showed it to be 2 centimetres wide.

It was a cauliflower-shaped growth in the throat, which seemed a good enough reason for Barry's chronic coughing. There was vague relief that the cause had been identified. But it failed to impress Barry, who seemed to be distracted. He appeared unable to absorb my description of the images displayed on the screen, focusing only on what he was required to do next. With little fuss we were directed back to the reception area.

This whole episode had a dreamlike quality, so outside our normal-day-to-day activities. We could almost have imagined it. But unfortunately it was very real. We were about to face some very hard facts.

4

Cause and Effect

I checked that Barry's 'hospital' bag included all essentials and that he had not forgotten anything. My inner talk was about staying calm, being supportive and caring, without being intrusive.

Usually I am quite practical, but now I felt a bit out of my depth. Learning about what we were dealing with was top of my list. I spent hours on the computer researching various aspects of this cancer and what I had discovered was only partially reassuring. Something that did have considerable impact was realising that this was a combined journey for everyone connected to Barry.

His family had rallied around and chased one another backwards and forwards on the phone, resulting in offers of help and pledges of support. Despite their own busy lives and schedules, they devised a workable program to assist. Barry and I were taken aback by their generosity of spirit, knowing that some old, complicated family history had to be overcome in order to carry out those promises of support. That history was put aside willingly. Barry became very emotional with gratitude and suddenly more appreciative of his family.

Most people would recognise the 'why me' scenario, and of course Barry questioned what was happening to him. Initially he wanted his diagnosis kept within the close family and he told me not to tell anyone. Was he in denial? He theorised loudly about his condition as he stridently paced the floor — it seemed that voicing various scenarios would help him make more sense of it all. Understandably so, as he is a broadcaster.

He obviously needed to work through and discuss what was going on inside him. He was impatient to identify the cause and was shaken to even consider a malignant growth may have taken root decades ago. His doctors indicated possible causes, involving smoking, relationships and alcohol usage, but as a non-smoker and social drinker he was not prepared to accept them and could not acknowledge any other causative effects such as genetic history. The uncomfortable uncertainty sat on him like a lead weight.

He questioned whether the many events he'd compered could have been detrimental to his health — in those days there had been little awareness of the impact of passive smoking. He recalled being in many smoke-filled venues, throwing up his hands as he remembered, as if to emphasise salient points. He reflected in disbelief that his health could have been affected by those past events.

There was also dismay about whether relationships, previous partners and casual encounters had in any way contributed to his current health crisis. According to some researchers, the HPV virus could be a likely culprit.

He certainly wasn't going to let alcohol be blamed for any of this — he wasn't a 'drinker' and had only drank moderately over the years. He's always enjoyed a social drink and wine with dinner: 'There's nothing wrong with that,' he stated.

How to deal effectively with his turmoil? Initially I played down the situation, skirting around his diagnosis and respecting his confidentiality. I could only listen and respond in whatever way seemed appropriate at the time. Parrying and deflecting his outbursts was emotionally exhausting. Maybe he just needed my attention, to bounce ideas and concerns off me. I decided that learning to sit quietly with him as he endured distress and uncertainty would be the best course of action. In stillness, the threads of connection between us were tangible, vibrating and tugging in our sharing. I was his companion, sharing the road — and feeling the pace slowing, I could be more true to whatever circumstances prevailed.

I did need to acknowledge that some things were beyond my control and I couldn't advise him about his health. It was unsettling and I felt it revealed my own shortcomings in the face of his anguish. It wasn't as if it could just be fixed and made better. Platitudes don't cut it either. Not wanting to be Pollyanna-ish, I admit to feeling buffeted by his outbursts and retreating into the garden at times. Birdsong was very soothing and the chattering and chirping in the treetops was quite restful.

Dealing with Barry's roller coaster of emotions was distressing and, being a companion on this journey with him, it was necessary to find some way of providing balance. The main thing I realised was that he was in an inner place that I could not go to. Despite wanting to support and help him, it was his personal situation. He was the one faced with finding a new perception of himself and deciding how he would transcend and resolve his current position.

He was the only person who knew exactly what he was going through.

He had said once that he would have followed his deceased partner Judy to the grave if he could, but had recognised it was not his time to go, even though it was hers. That was when his spiritual journey took a new direction. Now he was about to be tested — and only he could access his own inner core and strength. Only he could decide which form of treatment to accept. Only he could ponder and decide which way to go, after research, consultation with family and his medical team and a lot of meditation. He did that, knowing that whatever he decided, he had the full support and backing of us all. In the past, his family had questioned some of his motives and decisions, but now only he could call the shots.

I suggested to Barry that he might like to keep an audio diary of pertinent conversations with doctors, consultants, specialists and technicians. He was being bombarded with copious amounts of information and unable to really process what he'd been told. I could remember a lot of what he relayed to me, and could offer my own insights or questions to prompt him, but it wasn't as effective as a direct record. His memory let him down several times under the burden of so much data about different aspects of his condition. He didn't relate well to medical terminology at the best of times, so the audio diary was a definite bonus when he wanted to re-visit any necessary information. Having his son Matt accompany him to key consultations was a blessing as well, providing an invaluable sounding board. Matt's comforting presence was an immense support to Barry. And it was reassuring to me that he had bloke-to-bloke sharing.

Barry soon admitted that he'd been selfish in asking me to hide his diagnosis. Thanks to a conversation he'd had with his daughter Bec, he released me from the restriction of secrecy. Talking with her later was a significant turning point in my dealing with his distress. Her familiarity and professional training as a psychologist were indispensable, giving me the courage to travel the road ahead. She'd studied the correlation between physical and emotional suffering, and the emphasis on a positive attitude influencing wellbeing and recovery. What a relief to be able to speak more freely to the people who asked after him.

Barry's astrology sign is Cancer, the crab. Since he's an astrologer, we've usually spoken about cancer in the context of astrological significance. When faced with its medical version, our knowledge was very limited. Now we were on a steep learning curve. We associated his sun sign with far more benign homely influences. Cancerians can be moody, emotionally caring and protective. They can also have a tendency to want to take control, albeit with good intentions, thinking they know what's best for others (who may not always agree). So Barry found himself in a place where he really needed to access his own strengths, composure and discipline with self-management in mind.

It was a forty-five minute drive along the expressway towards the hospital at a prominent holiday destination on the Gold Coast. The sunny day was filled with small talk, admiring the scenery, commenting on the traffic conditions. Somehow we avoided mentioning what was up ahead. There was, after all, a serious edge to this trip.

Barry was having an operation on his throat — cutting a growth from his lingual tonsil — and for a broadcaster this was a big deal, a really big deal. There was a very real fear of not being able to talk on radio again, or even of never working again. No way was Barry ready for retirement. Being able to communicate and express himself is what he is all about. I wondered how he was going to approach such a major hurdle in his life.

But I needn't have worried. He has a powerful will to live and still has many things on his bucket list. One of his favourite expressions is 'I'm not going to die wondering'. So here was another milestone for him to traverse. He wouldn't be left wondering for long.

5

Hospital

Leaving Barry in the capable hands of the medical team seemed almost a cop-out. Of course, what could we do but wait until this operation was over. Matt and I drove off to spend companionable time strolling along the beachfront, then wandered into a café for a meal. Being able to talk through the cancer diagnosis and the ensuing treatment options with Matt was a relief. Neither of us could possibly know Barry's personal experience, but we did consider how much it might change his approach to life. It would probably rate as a 'worst life event' for him. It was not a time to dwell on the past, to blame or to regret decisions. Hopefully he would realise he can't change the past, accept what's happened and develop strategies for moving forward.

I probably prattled on far too much, releasing some of my pent-up tension. I'll always appreciate the way Matt was so calm and caring towards me, while showing concern about his father's condition. And in the background was his mother-in-law's ongoing battle with cancer. Matt's wife Claire had travelled to Britain to be with her mother and the whole family had pulled together. They have my greatest admiration for handling a difficult situation so competently.

Returning to the hospital was like entering another world. Recovering from the operation, Barry was being fussed over by the nurses and obviously appreciated their attention. He seemed oblivious to the paraphernalia surrounding him, including his soiled hospital garb. He tried to take charge of himself but, still being under the effects of the anaesthetic, didn't pull it off convincingly. Matt and I assisted, exchanging glances, silently acknowledging Barry's need for a bit more time to stabilise. We were pleased that his voice was definitely and gratifyingly audible.

The following is an excerpt from a message I sent out a few days later — it did feel like reporting from the 'news desk':

He stayed overnight for observation. When he returned home he quite easily managed a voiceover! He's recovering well, sore throat and slight hoarseness only needing Panadol for light pain relief.

He's now had pathology, and ultrasound tests show further treatment is required. The tests also showed up a multi-nodule goitre on his thyroid. Priority is being given to treating his tongue. He will be having an MRI on Sunday. Next Thursday (14th) he will travel to Brisbane Hospital (2 hour drive away) for further tests, and early Friday he will attend a panel discussion of experts regarding his ongoing treatment (accompanied by his son, as I need to return to Sydney). There's a possibility Barry will need radiotherapy treatment daily for the following 6 weeks.

....

Barry is handling it quite well, and has managed to retain his sense of humour so far.

6

Thyroid Removal

Once Barry was within the grasp of surgeons, it seemed hard to break away.

After the multi-nodule goitre on his thyroid was discovered, there were more tests and medical visits as well as family consultations. We also checked in with friends who had been through the process and lived without their thyroids for years — they were reassuring about the after-effects not being too restrictive.

One step at a time though, as initially only one side of the thyroid showed a positive test result indicating it needed to be removed.

Barry and I discussed the overall scenario, and his hunch was that the second side of the thyroid (with an inconclusive diagnosis) would likely cause no problems. He spoke to his family, who were orientated towards mainstream methods, as well as to medical experts, for advice. His dilemma was whether to follow logical medical procedures when intuitively he felt that it wouldn't all be necessary. Only he could decide which course of action to take, but in the event he felt bound to follow his family's expectations. In retrospect, he knows he didn't trust his gut feeling, which was to retain the second half of his thyroid gland. He has to live with that decision and the resultant effects of lifelong medication.

What he hadn't realised was the role the thyroid plays in controlling body temperature. The thyroid gland is part of the endocrine system and helps maintain the body's metabolism. Despite taking his daily medication, he has become very susceptible to feeling the cold. It's a good thing the weather in northern New South Wales is at least a couple of degrees warmer on average than Sydney.

When Barry decided to have the second half of the thyroid removed, the generosity of his surgeon Dr Tim knew no bounds. He offered to cut out an aggressive basel cell carcinoma which had suddenly erupted on his chest at the same time. I had returned to Sydney when Barry took to Skype to show me the ninja-shaped scar he now had decorating a large part of his chest.

7

What About Me?

Following his surgery, Barry became very anxious that I have a medical check-up myself. Old back problems had resurfaced and movement had become difficult, necessitating several sessions of remedial massage and acupuncture to smooth out the cricks. With some hesitation, I undertook a number of preliminary pathology tests. Areas of concern were revealed, which I downplayed so as not to concern him.

Barry became vehement about pursuing with all speed medical attention to two skin cancers on my face. I felt hassled, but realised that these small wounds that would not heal caused him a lot of anxiety. So, between Barry's operations and the commencement of his radiotherapy treatment, two carcinomas were removed from my forehead above my eye. Unfortunately, I didn't give myself sufficient time to properly prepare for the procedure and its painful consequences — but with all that Barry had been through, and was about to undertake, it felt selfish to focus on my own discomfort. After all, I was the carer and meant to be strong and supportive, and it would be seen as weakness to lean on someone else for comfort. At night, propped up with pillows and tossing and turning in pain, I tried to convince myself that it was nothing, a burden best borne alone in silence. The lop-sided facial disfigurement and bulky dressings didn't help to minimise the effect either. With ugly grotesque facial swelling, dark bruising and throbbing headache, I became averse to leaving the house. It really hurt, a lot. The scars are barely noticeable now, although memories of that awful procedure linger on.

Sometimes threads of human kindness connect in unexpected ways. Unable to wash my hair — the wounds had to be kept dry — I went to my usual hairdressing salon for assistance. They were wonderful, so kind and considerate, while giving gentle caring treatment and blow-drying my hair into a respectable look that eased my discomfort. I walked out feeling much better from being embraced in their goodwill.

8

Putting My Life on Hold

Leaving my home, family, pets, work and friends in Sydney for over two months to be with Barry during his radiotherapy treatments was a big thing for me. Much organisation was required — it wasn't a case of just dropping everything and walking out the door. I'm not sure that Barry fully realised the difficulties involved or the emotional impact it had on me.

A good friend moved into my house — workmen had been coming and going before she arrived, with crucial repair work still required. I had had to cancel a short trip to Western Australia which, regrettably, was not something that could be experienced later — it was for the eightieth birthday party of a life-long friend, almost a year in the planning. I was disappointed not to be able to share her special day with her. Customary employment obligations were cancelled despite the financial impact. There were also seemingly endless computer problems. Thankfully everything did eventually drop into place.

Then it was a rush getting to the airport, with thanks to my ex-husband Paul for ably navigating intense traffic conditions. Breathlessly I hurried to the ticket counter with minutes to spare. Alarmed at the thought of missing my flight, I rushed to the security gates and zigzagged through the crowds to the departure gate. My name was called out over the loud speaker. Hastily my ticket was accepted by the attendant and I was the last to board. Struggling down the aisle, my whole body trembling and pulsing, I thankfully found my aisle seat and wriggled my hand luggage into the overhead locker. With a huge sigh I finally flopped into my seat, fastened the seat belt and fell asleep. I don't remember anything of the eighty-minute flight.

At Brisbane airport, I managed to find the shuttle bus stop, boarded and vaguely considered my position as we headed goodness knows where. Everything felt like it was moving in slow motion. The bus driver spoke slowly, other passengers barely spoke at all and the peak hour traffic chugged along at snail pace. What was wrong with me? It felt like my perception of time had a kink in it. Maybe my own pace had ramped up with so much kerfuffle and my body needed to adjust to a more sedate speed.

Arriving at the rented apartment in the city was like being thrown in at the deep end — time to sink or swim. Barry was satisfyingly pleased to see me, which bolstered my flagging energy. He showed me around the neat two-bedroom apartment, before we headed out for dinner at the little Thai restaurant he'd discovered.

My introduction to the tomotherapy machine the following day was rather daunting. Claustrophobia struck just looking at it and I understood better how Barry felt. Seeing the mask he had to wear for each treatment was a surprise, as I'd imagined it to be solid and enclosing, especially since Barry had often referred to his anticipated panic about wearing it. The worst part was watching him being bolted to the platform base to prevent movement.

I questioned whether I could be the support person he so obviously wanted, but since the routines, schedules and transport were all in place, it quickly became apparent the concern was unnecessary. Barry and I had been in constant contact, and the routine was set to just follow established processes and treatment schedules. I was grateful that he had done so much prior preparation, including providing me with my own room — essential since his snoring resonated throughout the whole building. (A couple of years later, that's no longer a concern – an additional benefit of the whole procedure.)

I was more than willing to support Barry, and rose to the challenge. It would have been good nonetheless to have some recognition for having left so much of my everyday life behind, even though temporarily. By this stage, however, Barry's focus was on Barry, me as his companion and support, his doctors, his radiation treatment and all other associated links. My focus was to see him through the next couple of months with ease and to smooth out any lumpy bumpy obstacles — and make it seem effortless. Straightforward you'd think.

Barry was very considerate of my initial disorientation as we focused solely on hospital visits during the first couple of days. Late one afternoon he suggested we go exploring – wow, it was like unexpectedly being let out of detention.

We decided to investigate the area around the apartment, Spring Hill, to help orientate me in relation to the hospital and the city centre. It was a lovely way to wind down. We wandered past historic weatherboard cottages with pillared verandahs, fretwork and sash windows. These quaint colonial

1880s workers' cottages slowly came to life as the evening closed in, with soft-lit glows emerging from under the corrugated awnings. Farther along, a lofty mansion proclaimed its elegant heritage with patchwork stained-glass windows and a tall, elongated brick chimney on the peaked rooftop. Then we came upon the traditional Queenslander, exposed breezeway underneath, with compulsory slatted verandah surrounds and a tiny roof gable.

It can be so easy to get lost in a private bubble, losing sight of the immediate environment. Now was the time to close the door briefly on darker issues and open the door to brighter vistas. Seeing and feeling loveliness that evening as we strolled along companionably revealed our ability to respond to beauty, despite the feelings of numbness and distortion that were enveloping us. Here was the silver lining around the dark clouds. Focusing on beneficial influences and positive perceptions, rather than on what was lacking, was going to be important for the next few weeks.

Surely it wouldn't take much to adjust to the routine of daily hospital visits during each week in the city, with time out on the weekends at Barry's home in the country. Chuckling to myself, *I can do it*, gave me renewed energy and even put a bounce in my step. Revitalised, we meandered back to the apartment for an enjoyable dinner together.

9

Lull Before the Storm

My first weekend back at Barry's house in Mullumbimby was very relaxing after all the hustle and bustle of previous weeks. It was good to unwind in the countryside and just bask in a sense of timelessness. We took a lovely sunset walk along the misty beach at Brunswick Heads, a zephyr breeze faintly blowing my hair across my face, white sand crunching underfoot — it was liberating to see the turquoise ocean melding with endless aquamarine skies.

By now Barry was showing 'sunburn' effects from the radiotherapy, plus a dry sensitive throat affecting his swallowing, a loss of appetite and feelings of lethargy. He was in good spirits though, being relieved of the stress of the continual hospital processes during the week. It was great to see him at ease back home among his own things. He loved being able to stroll around his own overgrown subtropical garden, and wasn't overly upset when he suddenly became enmeshed in a bold spider's cantilevered web. It was all part of familiar territory. We browsed the uneven pathways, checking on favourite plants and gathering ripe passionfruit. We took note of fallen branches and compiled lists of future things to do.

Barry's excited call for me to quickly join him outside showed that magical moments can happen — the appearance of a three-metre long python on the wooden handrail of the back deck. Obviously safety was a priority and I wouldn't take needless risks, however I took the opportunity to creep slowly along her length taking photos. I trusted my immediate response of wonderment, which resulted in keeping a safe and respectful distance and not disturbing the python, while enjoying the mesmerising experience of enchantment. It was the Chinese year of the snake, which offered to give us all the opportunity to find inner strength and to have the courage of our convictions, resulting in personal empowerment. I've read that Native Americans believe that snakes shed their skin as a symbol of new beginnings. With such an auspicious visit from our own python, perhaps there would be a propitious new start ahead. Events like this demonstrate how the simplest things in life can be so life affirming, uplifting and sweetly sustaining.

It was wonderful to have such a great example of deeper awareness, of feeling heartfelt emotions resonating within, rather than on what 'ought' to be.

I began to muse about how we could choose to *respond* to enhancing opportunities, rather than to *react* sometimes defensively to those which seem detrimental. For instance, some people reacted very negatively when I told them about being up close to the python and questioned my sanity. Even Barry was concerned when I got too close for comfort, until he recognised that the snake was untroubled by my presence. Recognising and understanding the benefit of positive stimulus is vital to wellness I now believe. In this instance, I had no qualms about choosing my playmate of the day.

There are no expectations about how you *should* behave under those circumstances. If I'd been fearful, I expect the outcome would have been quite different. Anticipation of how life should be can limit greater opportunities. I've found that being open to positive happenings can improve the quality of experience and manifest positive outcomes — and I do need to remind myself of that from time to time.

When things are not proceeding well, I stop and reappraise: *what's going on inside?* It's not about running away from whatever is not working out. It's about creating a firm intention to generate a more improved or beneficial way forward — and then apply my motto: *there's always another way.*

Back in the garden again shortly after the snake visit, I saw a tawny frogmouth perched on the pool gate. It was sitting absolutely still and we wondered if it really was an owl or shadows forming an owl shape. In fact, it's not a true owl, but it looks like one – and I saw its appearance as symbolic. It was awesome to be able to be part of its environment, and even take a couple of photos. Elena Harris (http://www.spiritanimal. info/owl-spirit-animal/) refers to the owl connection with wisdom and intuitive knowledge — of seeing true reality, beyond illusion. Maybe I'll be inspired by wisdom through osmosis. 'When the owl shows up in your life pay attention to the winds of change …'

Mmmmm. Barry's cancer journey already indicated extensive changes. At a deep level, I felt that things would never be quite the same again, although that might not necessarily be a bad thing. Barry was definitely walking his path with due diligence now, even taking into account that he was always very good at being Barry, with all his foibles and personality traits.

Transitioning from our normal behaviour to dealing with cancer was inviting some serious soul-searching. Most likely changes in attitude would be motivated by reasons we hadn't previously thought of, or believed valid to us personally. Under duress, we may respond with alarm and make spontaneous lifestyle choices, which prove unsustainable once the crisis has abated, or allow old habits to reassert their influence.

With certain side effects such as sunburned skin, new habits had to be introduced to combat the pain. So covering up his neck and regular use of moisturising creams could end up creating long-term beneficial practices for Barry. His doctors had warned him that his radiation-burned skin would be extremely sensitive and to stay out of the sun. It set off a thoughtful review of habitual choices. Hail the use of a bandana neck scarf

One of Barry's favourite routines had been enjoying a glass of red wine with dinner, which is not something he's likely to want to give up permanently without very good reason. Soon after he started the radiation treatment, he found the taste of wine disgusting, although he fully expected his appreciation to be restored in due course. With such restrictions, social occasions would never be the same again for him. We'll see how that pans out over time — perhaps that will be the issue to provide further opportunities for changing personal behaviour patterns and creating new habits? I wondered how he would reward himself if treasured treats produced adverse consequences permanently.

Preparing meals for the week ahead soon became my routine on the weekends, and I'd usually freeze a couple of meals from the weekend to take back to the apartment too. Meanwhile, Barry took it easy, having quiet time with a good book, watching television, taking time out for revitalising meditation and rejuvenating healing sessions.

After the two-hour drive back to the apartment in Brisbane on a Monday, followed by a day full of hospital appointments, we were happy to settle back into the Spring Hill apartment late in the day. We'd then have a relaxing afternoon tea with probably a slice or two of the banana bread I'd made the day before.

On the days when he had an 8 am appointment, the whole day was left free. On one occasion Barry's two youngest granddaughters came to visit with their mum, and he delighted in providing treats for them and enjoying their company. We also enjoyed sharing a catch-up coffee and snack with his son Matt before he dashed off to start his radio shift at the nearby ABC studios. Family occasions such as this were very important to Barry during his treatment. I think it helped him realise the importance of including family in his life, having previously been primarily focused on his professional life. I think he'd agree that he hadn't always prioritised family, despite my promptings from time to time. Now I was seeing a very positive transformation, with him simply enjoying passing time with each family member. I hoped this would continue and have encouraged contact with them whenever possible.

Meanwhile in Sydney, strong winds had resulted in extensive damage in my local area, causing concern to my lovely house guest. But she assured me that in general everything was fine and only asked me to arrange some minor repairs. That was soon organised with many thanks to Paul's diligence, and before long everything was in order again.

Barry and I were wholeheartedly looking forward to a restful three-day holiday weekend coming up, followed by only four short days of treatment the following week. We couldn't get away from Brisbane quickly enough.

10

Long Weekend

The Queen's Birthday weekend in June stands out as the most alarming challenge over that two-month period for Barry and me. The discomfort of the 'sunburn' effect of the radiation treatment had turned into agonising pain. My heart turned over at the look of suffering on his face as he slumped forward in anguish. He'd taken off the used dressings and was waiting for me to put on new ones. The skin all round his neck and shoulders had ruptured with blisters, hot, fiery and thin as parchment. We only had moisturising cream given by the hospital and it was not effective in alleviating the pain. His skin was burned. It seemed only cool pads could dampen the heat to give minimal relief. I applied cream obtained from the local chemist gently and with as much 'healing' energy as possible. I wanted to hug him and smooth the hurt away. But that couldn't happen since the slightest pressure made him flinch in distress. So I continued smoothing the cream over his fragile skin, trying to caress the pain away.

I later fumed, just a little, that this *would* have to happen on the Friday night of a holiday weekend, at home in the country, two hours away from the hospital. No-one was close by to assist us, and familiar doctors were also away for the long weekend. Part of me felt peeved because the medical team hadn't warned me what to expect or anticipated that we'd reach this stage at this time.

It was frustrating to feel we didn't know enough to make a crucial decision about the best course of action to take. For some reason, I intuited that 'gel' was needed, although there was no information to back up my hunch. So for several hours over the next two days I channelled my sense of frustration into searching for answers or informative references on the internet.

There are multitudes of sites and forums offering great assortments of information and advice. Wading through it all showed me the enormous complexity of the medical and alternative approaches to cancer and related conditions. At times it was baffling and frequently required academic prowess beyond my capabilities. Snippets of information would occasionally seem relevant and in discussion we'd bounce the ideas around, usually concluding limply with *why don't we mention it at the hospital next week*. Although I did persevere with the research, it was tiring and Barry seemed to tune out, going into his own inner space to escape it all.

I changed Barry's dressings daily, each time feeling an unexpected cocoon of intimacy as together we huddled over his painfully burned skin and rupturing blisters. He tentatively shared that he didn't want to be a burden to anyone. He referred to people he knew who were dependent on others for care and said that he couldn't bear to be like that. Being incapacitated to him meant loss of personal dignity. Of course that was not necessarily so, although not an option he could contemplate at that time.

I wasn't used to him revealing his vulnerability. He'd always been rather assertive and very much in charge of his own destiny. I felt unexpectedly reserved at his humility. He was apprehensive about how his condition could affect others. It was a big uneasy step outside his comfort zone. An invisible barrier had been breached.

Strangely, my mood improved. I felt better not having to second guess Barry's state or being perturbed by his hidden emotions and not fully understanding the reasons why. It felt like just being open to the question with no hidden agenda — a mystery to be lived, not a problem to be solved.

I gently reassured him that he wasn't a burden to me, and no-one else had indicated that he was either. What were the real messages, emotions and beliefs being courageously expressed from his vulnerable state? Connecting at a genuine level was important, rather than regressing into guilt about his condition. Listening with caring became the healing balm that soothed away tiresome and painful echoes of distress. Our bond deepened.

We were beyond limp platitudes of *it'll be right mate*. Quiet time was indispensable for us both. He needed to retreat into his 'cave' to regenerate occasionally. It was all he had to fall back on to sustain him through the brunt of his pain — waiting in despair was not his style. He just needed to feel he was back in the driver's seat.

Somehow we managed to get through that very long, nerve-wracking weekend and he was literally back in the driver's seat on the Tuesday, heading back to the city and straight to the hospital.

Because of the agonising deterioration of his skin, the treatment did change to include 'gel'. It was effective almost immediately, much to our great relief. The nursing staff showed me how to apply a gel dressing pad, and it remained my primary job on the weekends, and other times when necessary. The wisdom in the words of the American psychologist Virginia Satir was certainly relevant: 'Life is not the way it's supposed to be. It's the way it is. The way you cope with it is what makes the difference.'

Barry wanted to make amends for 'spoiling our long weekend' — not that he had, and not that it was necessary, but it was a lovely gesture. We both happily anticipated an outing to give us respite from the limitations his schedule imposed on us — in other words, we were ready for a 'break out'. He arranged a delightful day trip away from the hospital and city to the Sunshine Coast, north of Brisbane, to meet his brother and sister-in-law for lunch. It was lovely to be greeted by their smiling faces and warm hugs. We enjoyed wandering through an eclectic art gallery in Montville and driving around the countryside in one of my all-time favourite picturesque locations. It was such a refreshing day out, embraced and sustained by family, nourishment and nature. We returned to the apartment tired and content. The 'Sunshine' Coast lived up to its name that day.

Back in Brisbane we were adjusting to the changes, but it did take its toll. I was infected by a virus — and that was the last thing we needed. I had tried to ignore the sore throat, headache, snuffles, muscular aches and pains, saying it was probably just an allergy. But I couldn't ignore a full-on dripping nose, sneezing and throbbing headache — all I wanted was a hot bath and bed. Concerned that a virus would further compromise his health if passed on, I kept my distance from Barry. That didn't work, although luckily he ended up only mildly affected. It looked like his immune system was in better shape than mine. In a way it was a relief to succumb. I just felt miserable.

I remembered the hospital waiting room being unusually noisy with many people coughing. The receptionist confirmed there was a 'bug' going round, with many staff struck down as well as patients. She said most were affected for about four days. That wasn't what we wanted to hear. Each day we had deliberately sat away from the main waiting room crowd, hoping to avoid any contagions. By this stage Barry and I had favourite seats, his being a nice, big comfy armchair. While Barry faced the tomotherapy machine, I usually browsed magazines — perhaps they had harboured colonies of germs. With all the comings and goings in the area, I guess it was no wonder 'bugs' had taken hold and been transported among us.

There was a table of three young women grouped near us one day, all wearing turbans of different styles and colours, one of them frail and slumped in a wheelchair. They were chattering and giggling among themselves, pointing out fashion favourites in the glossy magazines, seemingly oblivious to anything out of the ordinary about the location. I was impressed by the normality of them gathering as if they were 'meeting for coffee'. I hoped they would avoid the random bugs taking over the space and continue to embrace the obvious pleasure they experienced together. Long-lasting friendships can be cemented by sharing difficult times.

It prompted me to think of their peers, who could possibly be very awkward in this hospital setting. Feeling inadequate and uncomfortable in the face of unexpected life-threatening illness would affect most people, regardless of age. It may only need to be acknowledged with something like *I don't know what to say*, or sometimes silence and companionable sharing is all that's needed. We don't always know how to respond appropriately. Just knowing someone is there, is caring enough to be there, can be very reassuring to someone grieving about their potential loss of health and 'normality'.

In our case, in the face of a confronting diagnosis, becoming detached from routines, familiar surroundings and people caused a sense of isolation. From my perspective, standing back to give people space is not always the optimum way of dealing with the situation either. It's about being supportive throughout a time of difficulty and suffering.

We'd been looking forward to the coming weekend, a change of scenery, passing time at the local markets and responding to two social invitations, one of which was a 'healing' session for Barry. Any or all of those activities would have been beneficial to help take our mind off other complex matters. However, I was confined to recovery mode, and had no desire to go out and about or inflict my ill health on anyone else.

How often have we heard about people going away for a break and then coming down with the flu? It seems it's all to do with the immune system's response to stress, whether we're stressed out with our hectic day-to-day activities or rushing around getting frazzled organising a trip away. I've read that once we've de-stressed a little, the stress response hormone cortisol becomes less active, causing the immune system to function below par until it readjusts. That's when we're most likely to pick up random bugs. Best remedy? For me — get plenty of sleep. And stress less.

11

Halfway Point

Tensions had increased. The continued pressure of hospital visits was taking its toll on both of us and differences in personality became more pronounced. Customary roles were changing and strains between patient and carer perspectives became apparent. Meeting the increasing needs of the treatment, both emotional and physical, as well as of each other in the enclosed environment of the small unit was demanding. We were both unsettled by being away from the stability of our own homes. Trying to balance 'normal' with unusual and unexpected extremes was becoming more difficult. Something had to give, and it did — loudly and vocally, we expressed our anguish and aggravation.

Airing heated grievances at pressure-cooker level was really not the best choice of action. However, not owning them would most likely have produced further eruptions and irrational angry outbursts.

It began innocently enough with a bland comment about finances. Each of us obviously needed to express our point of view to the other. This escalated into a kaleidoscope of scenes and our equilibrium was about to be shattered under close scrutiny. In retrospect, maybe the issues could have been aired differently, or with a more considerate tone of voice, or somehow moderated not to cause offence. However, in all probability, it seemed nothing would have made the slightest difference. It was as if the volatile situation had created its own energy and stood all powerful between us, poised to erupt.

There was of course a history, a story behind it, with unresolved long-term issues — that, in fact, were not only of our own making. There really was no answer, no resolution and no obvious course of action. It was from the past. We couldn't do anything to change what had happened. What we really needed to do was acknowledge our pain, and accept and reconcile our differences about the way the past was affecting us now. We did that, although sadly not at all in a conciliatory way.

That's when it became obvious we needed to take time out. My motto, there's always another way, well and truly needed to be activated. We were both hurting about a current situation that had a different source for each of us. We had wrongly assumed we could force a change in each other's perspective. Did 'being right' really matter so much? Feeling vulnerable and stressed, we had each succumbed to flawed default positions. Our true natures and inner selves needed an opportunity to be expressed here, to reveal innate kindness, acceptance and understanding.

After time out — I striding out, breathing deeply, on an hour-long walk among a nearby copse of trees, he sitting quietly in reflection — with yet another hospital appointment looming, we both calmed down and returned to face each other. This time we talked quietly, sharing, and listening attentively.

We always have a choice about how to respond to any situation. Once we'd quietened, we were able to voice our opinions, share perspectives and acknowledge our differences. We recognised there was no blame on either side. Strange that in the greater scheme of things, it was not really our differences that mattered. Our minds can talk us into and out of anything. We'd become separated from our physical reality by becoming engrossed in past associations. Let it be. What became apparent and most important was the genuine consideration we were able to show each other.

Barry shared the results of his reflections, making a conciliatory gesture and showing he had a better understanding of the situation. I met this with acceptance of our shared dilemma, recognising our joint efforts were the best way forward. With tentative reconciliation, emotional energy drained and antagonism spent, we moved towards each other. We hugged, *very* gently.

We both felt the strain of our outburst as we made our way to the hospital shortly afterwards. As it was a fine day, walking instead of catching the bus eased us into a mellow mood. Somehow we were more companionable with each other. I felt more compassionate towards the physical discomfort he was experiencing with his angry reddened skin, general health issues and the distress it caused him. As the tension abated, it almost seemed like we were emerging from a 'storm in a tea cup'.

Neither of us wanted to be caught up in noisy traffic, so we headed towards the welcoming open space and greenery of a nearby park. It was a relief to be outside and nurtured by nature. I noticed my footsteps were in companionable rhythm with Barry's. My vision and perceptions were clearer.

We passed two men exercising in the park and shared a quiet joke about fitness enthusiasts. Further on we asked a couple walking towards us for directions. They obliged with willing smiles. Only as we turned to continue on our way did we appreciate that the frail, slightly stooped figure of the man in loosely hanging clothing was most likely undergoing some form of medical treatment himself.

Almost at the hospital, we needed to check again for directions. The hospital is in a park-like setting with numerous buildings. Approaching from the park instead of by bus meant entering through unfamiliar pathways that twisted and turned between multistorey buildings. This time, directions were cheerily given by a vibrant woman with medical qualifications (indicated by an identity tag). She was obviously aware of the exactness required to navigate the area, firmly pointing out steps and pedestrian crossings we'd soon be encountering. We thanked her and continued as directed.

Finally entering the oncology building, we stopped at a cafeteria with a good selection of snacks available, as well as more substantial hot meals. Our mood, having been a little subdued with the lingering after-effects of our conflict, lightened. We chose our food, found an outside table, and settled into a closeness that almost defied our previous unsatisfactory encounter.

Barry spied a bird foraging for crumbs on the patio nearby. He threw a piece of his lunch towards it. Suddenly there was a flutter of wings and several birds descended, each jostling to retrieve the morsel. Encouraged by their enthusiasm, Barry sent several more scraps among them, laughing as they scrounged for their own morsel. Happily they all seemed satisfied with their portion, and Barry's equilibrium was restored. We were back on an even keel — at least as far as we could be for now. What a relief.

12

Later the Same Day

Around us were diverse types of people, all in their own little bubbles. We were all in a hospital for medical-related reasons. They were all influenced by their own stories, their own issues and their own ways of being.

Sitting under cover on the patio, protected from the direct sun, was a family group. Adults and older children gathered round a young girl in a wheelchair with a bandana on her sparsely haired head. Her eyes looked mature beyond her age, possibly not fully understanding the firm expressions of her parents. As she was chatting, the adults and older siblings, more observers than participants, were hanging on to the changing palette of her appearance, as if to fix the memory firmly into their consciousness.

Not far away was a group of solidly built young adults, struggling to find a table. Bumping into chairs, scraping them across the concrete and noisily disturbing adjoining patrons, they scattered all before them and settled unceremoniously into seemingly undersized seating.

Not noticing this disruption, an elderly man was assisted to a seat several tables away. With a stick to steady him, the help of his wife and the brisk management of his daughter, he sank with a grimace into his seat. His wife fussed over him, while his daughter stood sentinel-like to take his lunch order. She seemed impervious to anything else, including her father's discomfort. Once her mother had given instructions about the food, she departed with purpose towards the café interior. Her parents' drooping shoulders indicated weary suffering.

As the time for Barry's appointment drew closer, we headed towards the radiation department. Along the way, we passed an isolated woman sitting stock still at a tiny information desk. Barry stopped to pass the time of day with her, sensing that she might appreciate company — she seemed so alone and detached. Perhaps she echoed a loneliness he was familiar with. She looked like she'd been daydreaming and was a little flustered at his attention. I felt we were intruding on her space. We smiled and continued.

There were other service tables, gift shops, noticeboards, departmental reception areas, coffee carts and lounge areas in a large foyer area that we had to pass through. Turning off along a corridor, our attention was drawn to an exhibition of Aboriginal paintings on the walls. The colours and shapes were a welcome enticement to linger. I felt the warmth of the tradition and wondered if the artist had intended to include a healing element in the paint work.

As the doors of the lift opened to take us to the third floor, we noticed a bright-eyed older man with a stick hurrying as best he could to catch the lift. We held it for him. He confidently and proudly shared with us that it was twelve months since the end of his treatment and that he was only there for a check-up. He got out at the wrong floor, but despite his difficulty walking, he was unphased at the detour, and with cheerful good humour retraced his steps. I remarked to Barry that he was a great example of someone who had gone through the struggle, come out at the other end and survived with good cheer intact. With good grace, that old man was happy to smile and share with others. He certainly lifted my spirits.

Each observation of the different groups of people that day struck a chord in me, especially the raw emotional connections. My awareness was activated and I felt able to see outside my own bubble and appreciate that everyone was walking their own individual journey, in a shared community environment — all somehow connected to that specific hub of buildings at that point in time. That was a liberating concept, quite different from my usual perspective. I had come face to face with a mixed bunch of people that day and met them head on in the midst of an extraordinary moment. What a gift.

After the treatment we decided to catch a bus back from the hospital to the city centre, a ten-minute trip. We did a little 'breakout' shopping and then joined a long bus queue. It was the end of the working day, and eventually we boarded a crowded bus and gratefully found some seats. Nearby was a window seat occupied by a handbag and next to that, in an aisle seat, was a coiffed, well-dressed fifty-year-plus woman with a stern face studiously ignoring the file of people looking at her handbag. As the bus became packed, she took the bag onto her lap but didn't budge. Even when an elderly couple struggled aboard, she didn't move — luckily others gave up their seats for them. In a packed bus, the whole aisle squeezed tight with standing passengers, one isolated woman hogged two seats, not sharing or caring. Barry was incensed when he noticed her selfishness. His fragile condition seemed to magnify his reaction. He was quite verbal when she got off at the same bus stop as us and muttered his way into our apartment building, not caring if she heard his comments.

We'd experienced a roller-coaster ride of emotions that day, which had evolved into mutual awareness and sensitivity. We'd learned much from our 'failure' in communication. As we went up in the lift to our unit, it was as if we were entering a protected cocoon. We were eagerly anticipating the treat of a tasty Asian takeaway meal.

Glad to be free from having to cook, I just wanted time out to retreat with a good book after dinner. Barry anticipated watching the television for a bit of escapism.

We both got what we needed and slept unexpectedly soundly.

13

Nine Days to Go

Barry thought a walk into the city would be a good way to start the day and get some exercise, given that we had five hours before his treatment. Walking along the Mall in the city centre, we saw Queensland's State of Origin team having fun doing a boisterous publicity appearance before the big game against New South Wales. I pulled Barry close to the stage, thinking it might brighten his day to be part of the action. It was great to see him enjoy it so much.

At the hospital later, Barry jauntily greeted Connie, his oncologist nurse, on his way to face the tomo machine again. He returned to see her thirty minutes later for a special dressing to be applied. Connie took us to a curtained cubicle and cheerfully set about attending to his very fragile skin. She bantered with Barry as usual, making fun of the white-collared style of his neck dressing, alternating comments about the royal 'Elizabethan' style, and the white-collar 'priestly' style she was creating. We joked about using dressmaking skills with today's dressing and making comparisons of cutting skills so the 'yoke' fitted snugly. She explained the importance of fitting the dressing properly so it stayed on and protected his neck and shoulders. We were jovial, but it was a necessary practical issue.

The humour extended into hearty laughing, drawing other nurses to peek around the curtain to see what all the frivolity was about. Barry was due to meet with Jenny and Susan, the speech therapist and dietician respectively, and we were running late for the appointment. They came looking for us, heard Barry's laugh, and tracked us down to the noisy cubicle. When they poked their heads between the curtains, they also burst into laughter at the sight of Barry being swathed in white strips of dressing fabric, with Connie endeavouring to cover the wide area of skin damage with a protective dressing. Cutting the right length and draping it effectively over his broad shoulders was proving to be a complicated matter. Two heads withdrew, still chuckling, saying they'd return in ten minutes.

By the time they came back, we were still laughing with barely controlled mirth. We had been working out how to stabilise the dressing, once the 'yoke' started to take shape around his shoulders. Not wanting to delay further, we invited them into the inner 'sanctum', suggesting we conduct our meeting behind closed curtains instead of behind closed doors. They squeezed into the crowded cubicle and produced notebooks.

Susan and Jenny asked about Barry's meals and eating issues. Being serious proved to be far too difficult and we collapsed into almost-hysterical laughter at his appearance. There he was, tarted up with his neckpiece and yoke cut to measure and completing the 'look' with white figure-hugging boob tube. It was all too much. We clutched our sides aching with so much laughing. Laughter really is the best medicine — and that day it proved to be such a therapeutic release.

The Joy of Living

The following evening we were watching the news program *The Project* on TV featuring the 'Love Your Sister' story of Samuel Johnson. I was emotionally moved by the way he had embarked on a 15,000-kilometre journey to ride a unicycle around Australia to raise awareness of breast cancer. His sister Connie had already fought three bouts of cancer. What started as a joke between them turned into the toughest challenge she could set for her brother. For Samuel, it was all about raising a million dollars for breast cancer research, raising awareness of the disease that was killing Connie and breaking the Guinness world record for the longest distance on a unicycle (which is 'a pedal-driven device kept upright and steered by body balance', which makes the sheer magnitude of Samuel's undertaking impressive). On screen was the reunion in Perth of this brother and sister who were battling her cancer together (see www.loveyoursister.org). There was a big crowd to welcome and applaud them, many tears, much laughter and lots of hugging. My tears flowed with theirs as easily as if I was with them, although it was all happening 4000 kilometres away on the other side of Australia. But I felt I was with them in spirit as Perth was my home town. I cried for their dedication to each other, strong family ties, generous fundraising and community support. In my own raw emotional state, I connected with the love and compassion surrounding their amazing journey.

14

Incidentally …

My flu symptoms came back and I felt dreary, with a croaky voice seemingly empathising with Barry's. By now I was also feeling a bit frustrated with being cooped up week by week, only traipsing between the apartment and the hospital. I tried to keep busy, popping into the Mall at times for an hour's distraction. We went to the cinema to see at least one movie a week, choosing something light and/or humorous to help keep our spirits up. Barry enjoyed scanning the local newspapers or internet for the latest film release and reviews. He would discuss the merits of the options on his shortlist, then we'd choose whichever session best fitted into the treatment schedule.

Keeping a selection of books close also helped us withdraw when needed. Quiet times were essential to keeping us on a level plane, something I would recommend for anyone in the same situation.

The radiation effects on Barry's taste buds were especially vexing when it came to choosing food that he found even halfway edible. Anything hot and spicy was a definite no-go. Barry had always loved a good hot curry and now he could barely tolerate anything even slightly spicy. Losing his sense of taste meant he didn't really appreciate what he was eating — and didn't feel that anything much was appealing, nourishing or nutritious. It resulted in him eating less. It would have been okay if he intentionally intended to lose weight, which would have been good for his overall health, but not under these conditions. At times we'd go out looking for something appetising for dinner, hoping to find anything inspiring (something that would bring a spark of appreciation), but we were not always successful,.

Early on Barry had taken me to the charming family-owned Thai restaurant he'd found before my arrival. There was a lovely woman he wanted me to meet. She had a big welcoming smile and exuded homeliness. Barry felt her wholesome goodwill as if a warm embrace. She appeared to like the company of everyone around her. Her special gift to diners, besides her delightful cuisine, was her positive vitality. Some believe that when a cook or chef is passionate about their food creations, it has a discernible impact on the dishes they produce — their cheerful good mood is transferred by vibration to the food, which is then absorbed by the diner, who receives the positive nourishing energy. Was that an expanded glow surrounding us? We were happier and stronger after enjoying her company and our delicious meal with her family.

One of life's lessons is about our choice to be with people who lift us up or drag us down. Barry made an excellent choice with that restaurant.

A little later we were saddened by news of my seventeen-year-old cat's passing in Sydney, coincidentally at the same age and exact location — and as peacefully — as her beautiful loving Siamese mum two years earlier. She had been so close to death at one stage during the previous year that the vet had suggested putting her down, an unbearable notion. My daughter Tanya had nursed her, loving her back to us for another twelve months and embracing her recovery. Also vital to the rescue effort was the tender care and efforts of my other daughter Kat and my grandson Caiden. Memories of loving snuggle times with my gorgeous pets swamped my feelings. Images of my daughters and grandson playing with them were wistfully nostalgic. I was missing them, lots. I felt adrift. I was missing being close to my family. They were setting up in new locations and I felt very much out of the loop.

Still later, Barry and I chatted about mundane domestic matters, including the importance of companion animals. Barry had previously enjoyed the company of his own black cat Apollo, who was eminently suited to the role of an astrologer's assistant. Sadly he'd passed shortly before Barry moved away from Sydney. Barry had felt bereft, but had been reluctant to replace him since he'd expected to be away from his new home periodically.

One afternoon we wandered casually through shopping arcades, glancing at colourfully decorated displays and gathering a few necessities along the way. We were heading towards the supermarket. Riding up an escalator with Barry one step below me, I suddenly felt his arms creep around me — and embrace me very gently. He whispered softly against my hair, 'By the way, I really do love you.' Almost melting with tenderness at his unexpected declaration, it was as if time stood still as we were effortlessly conveyed to a higher level. Arriving at the next level, we nestled in cherished intimacy and stepped off in unison. We resumed our trip to the supermarket, arms entwined in the gentlest hug, enclosed in our personal bubble and oblivious to the very public domain, our spirits contentedly elevated.

That moment commenced a chain of agreeable changes. The way of understanding our 'relationship' from 800 kilometres apart now had different connotations. So maybe we're not boxed into a conforming arrangement. Maybe after thirteen years it's time to consider different ways of connecting.

Barry had become far more affable, his demeanour softened and a new willingness to compromise emerged — not so much of the 'I'll do it my way' mindset.

15

Introspection

With only two days until the final tomotherapy treatment, Barry became serious. He wanted to talk about an insight he'd written about in his books on the afterlife. Its significance was to fully realise and accept that his body was not really him. The *real* Barry was his soul, which he believes oversees what happens to his body. This perception led to us having a deep discussion, which I guess is not surprising when facing challenging life and death issues.

We talked about how the personal sense of ourselves varies, according to different circumstances. We could see how our behaviour changed when we interacted with different people — for example, depending on our perception of whether others approve of us or not. Maybe when we feel inadequate we compromise our values and behaviour to become more acceptable in a superficial way. We might change again when in another location or when other circumstances changed. In order to be sincere, to be poised and authentic, means to understand how we are drawn out as if by magnets into the world 'out there'. It's possible to see how our thoughts can take us randomly to the point of daydreaming, where it might even seem as if we're sleepwalking through our daily activities. How has the soul become veiled?

We talked about how our thoughts can lead us into and out of anything, as we make seemingly rational decisions and choices, often distorting any semblance of *real* truth, especially when we're subject to even the slightest stress. How can we even know what is real in such a confusing and baffling condition? When head or mind energy scurries every which way, our actions and emotions follow, tumbling reactively all over the place. How can anyone even say 'I' when they are truly made up of a myriad of complicated and bewildering parts, with each aspect of their personality reacting moment by moment to a variety of stimuli. It is possible to see people doing an apparent about turn and becoming contradictory and controversial even to themselves when not maintaining a consistent persona.

Using the word 'I' with discretion and perception can broaden and intensify our approach to matters that we consider important, even briefly, maybe even with inspiration. This way our *recognition* of what's possible can consolidate into a more solid core of soul-awareness. Who is the 'I' calling the shots in our own life? 'Be yourself; everyone else is already taken', a quote attributed to Oscar Wilde, illustrates this point.

A sincere understanding of our own weaknesses can influence our sympathy, tolerance and compassion for others who are not so fortunate, as Barry and I had already discovered on this unexpected journey. Maturing changes were already occurring naturally. As a result of facing and overcoming obstacles and challenges, we became aware of the potential to draw on, develop and strengthen our innate characteristics. It did mean taking risks and exposing our vulnerability, and it seemed we were up for the challenge.

Barry's observation about the importance of his soul's direction suggested a deeper and usually hidden part of him waking up in the face of his struggle with cancer. His intense striving to understand and overcome the disease was very much in his favour, using the very powerful tool of his intention to contract his energy into a laser-like focus (not unlike the tomotherapy). He seemed to realise it was time to bring in all possible resources and make them count. It takes sincere courage to peep out from behind an established mask.

16

Changing World

Politics ruled the second last day of Barry's treatment. In the nation's capital there was turmoil in the ranks of those in power. Big confrontations over who was going to win the ballot for the leadership dominated the news headlines. However, it was business as usual at the reception desk when Barry showed up for his appointment. It was surprising that his normally keen interest in current affairs was not evident. He seemed unconcerned by the political squabbles of the day, focusing only on his next tomo session.

Barry was more confident as he went through the now-familiar process, despite the pain he was experiencing. He even started to farewell and say thanks to various staff members, who he might not see before the final session. My emotions fluttered as we found 'our' seats. Almost buoyantly he responded to the call to attend the treatment room. The Time Lord was watching the clock like never before, definitely on a countdown.

Afterwards, we went off to treat ourselves to a magnificent Movenpick ice-cream indulgence. Ordinarily we'd not even consider such extravagance. However, with the soreness in

Barry's mouth, his choice of treats was limited and ice cream was now at top of the list for soothing his discomfort. Even the nutritional advisers had encouraged this developing addiction because they wanted him to maintain his weight. So we celebrated the impending completion of the tomo radiation by tucking into mounds of delicious ice cream. It had become his comfort food.

In the background, television reporters were having a field day with rumours and conjecture over who would be the next prime minister as they waited for the ballot numbers. Barry showed more interest in his ice cream than with affairs of the nation.

Months later, Barry's freezer was jammed with various containers of differing brands and flavours of ice cream, which caused great concern when he realised how addicted he'd become. Coconut had been his long-time favourite flavour and he rarely resisted an opportunity to indulge. Strangely, in the following months it prompted the use of organic coconut oil, with its suggested cleansing properties, as a mouthwash. Over time it also helped beat sugar cravings. After many years of being overweight, he was glad that his coconut phase aided much-needed weight loss.

He rationalised his continuing dependency on ice cream by recalling that the nutritionist had encouraged the habit, so he wouldn't lose weight, notwithstanding his own common sense telling him he was overdoing it.

17

Going Home

At the hospital, 8 am, 27 June 2013. One more dressing. 'Today's a bit of an anti-climax,' Barry had said and his mood was rather flat.

He returned to the unit from hospital with yet another dressing around his neck — we thought he'd finished with that. His shoulders were blistering slightly and needed cream to soothe the itchiness. The white cravat look had returned.

His coughing was still very pronounced, coarse, sounding like a fog horn. Bouts of it triggered my wincing reaction. I had to clamp my teeth to avoid comment or exclamation. It's one of those personal things — the intensity and unexpectedness of the strident noise really jarred me and I felt out of balance. How wretched he must have been feeling to cough so wholeheartedly, and repeatedly, his throat inflamed and scarred from the operation, his neck burned by the radiation. Of course he needed my compassion, which was darn hard to do through gritted teeth. I had to take a moment and step back. Deep breathe, into the stomach. My inner talk was, *fill up with gratitude. He's walked through all the treatment idiosyncrasies so far. I'm with him whatever the way.*

Hauling suitcases and paraphernalia carefully down slippery stairs to the underground carpark for the last time soon had us back on track. We didn't want to risk a fall when we were about to escape the urban confines.

With relief, we navigated congested traffic through light rain, driving cautiously out of the city. Halfway home we stopped at a large shopping complex. We became squished into crowded aisles full of folks furiously negotiating the half-year sales. The noise of squeaky trolleys loaded with bargains irritated Barry as they bumped past him, only just managing to be manoeuvred by harried parents. Bumptious children chattering and skipping along were exhilarated to be on holiday. The raucous hubbub intruded on clear thinking. What was needed next? He couldn't think straight. Barry visibly began to wilt. He was searching for a scarf, cravat or bandana — anything that would protect his neck from abrasive shirt collars and any sort of hot weather effects, particularly sunburn. Unenthusiastically he purchased a lightweight silken scarf and started to grumble about the crowds. Suddenly his resistance crumbled, the din overwhelmed him and he had to get out of the shopping centre, fast We scuttled to the nearest exit, not sure we would even find the car. We did.

I drove. He dozed. Soothing rain lightly drummed on the car roof.

Reorientating ourselves at home was a simple process. It was reassuring to pack our provisions away in the pantry instead of into a transitory box or bag. Barry repeatedly said how wonderful it felt to be home. He went from room to room, sharing comments about little details as he revisited familiar territory.

The next day, he wandered around vaguely, saying he was feeling the homecoming to be a bit of an anticlimax. The various things I suggested that might interest him mostly brought a lacklustre response.

Not forgetting 'me time', I took off on a long walk to refresh and catch up on exercise. I'm grateful for kindly advice, emphasising the need for carers to maintain their welfare and wellbeing. It could be so easy to get lost in the patient's issues to the detriment of the carer. Personal nurturing can easily be relegated to the bottom of the list when life events take a detour into difficult times. I needed to stay on track for myself and be nourished spiritually, as well as in the role of a compassionate functioning carer.

On my return Barry was ensconced in a phone conversation with a long-time friend. Catching up later, he couldn't remember much — he said they were just chatting, nothing meaningful, just talking. Few details of the chat seemed to have stayed with him, which concerned me a little.

He drifted along and became indifferent for a while as he readjusted to life outside the tomotherapy routine. I can't say adjusting back to 'normality' here, as our idea of normal only vaguely resembled life before tomo.

Note to self: Help him find an anchoring place again. Time to return to planet earth.

18

Readjustment

What brings a smile to Barry's face? What activities or interests have brought him pleasure and fulfilment throughout the years? What sustains him, reaffirms him and centres him inside, what gives him a sense of both feet on the ground?

He still enjoyed tennis. A few days after completing treatment, still coughing copiously, he obviously wasn't ready to 'have a hit'. His response to my suggestion that he might pop into the midweek game for a social chat was dismissive and off hand.

I missed my cuddly white fluffy dog still in Sydney. We would normally walk twice a day, especially enjoying our more leisurely evening ramble. One chill evening I was again lonely in his absence as I strolled along a quiet country road. I pulled my jacket close against a nippy puff of wind. There was a faint smell of wood burning in the air. Below me in the valley was a wispy trail of smoke lightly filtering from a thin chimney stack. It hovered over a homely cottage, making lazy random patterns against the backdrop of trees. Then, out of the dusky sky, silhouetted against silvery veils of distant clouds, flew a perfect V formation of birds. Silently they headed towards me, swerving, changing course, avoiding the smoke, realigning, gliding in single file above. It was awesome to share their twilight excursion. Smiling farewell to them, I continued walking into the chilly evening, and felt rejuvenated by the time I returned to the house.

Meanwhile, what else would help to settle Barry?

Being an astrologer, maybe information about the 'super moon' would interest him. Like many locals, we'd been on the beach to view the winter solstice moonrise the previous week. As we'd passed the village pub, inside an upbeat band had begun playing a rousing version of 'Oh What a Night'. We were almost tempted to step into dance mode. At the beach, families and small groups huddled around glowing campfires to keep warm. The horizon was obscured by beautiful pink-hued clouds, reflected in shallow waves on the smooth sandy shore.

Moonrise came and went, unseen, obscured by clouds. Dusk closed in. In the evening chill, people hugged warm garments close. Somewhere, as the night darkened, a low intimate drumming throbbed. As we drove away, we finally glimpsed the glowing full moon, cresting the cloud bank briefly, beaming a huge smile, then mischievously disappearing behind darkened clouds to go about its business.

With rain settling in and weather temperature dropping, Barry began musing about comfort foods. He wanted broth soup. None in the pantry so, despite the wind and wet, we bustled back to the car and took off in search of it or a suitable substitute. Finding nothing remotely like he wanted, I searched the refrigerated shelves for stock bones. I would make stock and turn it into good old-fashioned soup.

Making the soup was fairly time-consuming and I pottered about the kitchen happily. It was pleasing to be engrossed in peeling and chopping vegetables. Reaching the point of final flavouring, I grated lemon, added salt and flavouring, threw in a little finely chopped fennel leaf, stirred it and presented him with a spoonful for taste testing. Barry had always been so particular about flavour that it had become a habit to get his verdict before serving. So even with his mouth ulcers, sore throat, and coughing, it still felt important to continue the ritual. (There had already been one dish that had met with sharp rejection. Apologising, he'd asked me not to take it personally — he just hadn't been able to eat it.) Luckily the taste test on this occasion hit his taste buds with a satisfying sigh, 'Oh yes.' The soup was just what he needed — comfort food.

Accepting a social invitation for a meal was definitely out of the question. He was very conscious of his dilemma and chose not to inflict his condition on an unwary host or hostess. Indeed, he was too embarrassed by his vulnerability to put even close family and friends to the test.

Getting back to astrological matters, my thoughts turned to interesting facts relating to the term 'super moon' — how it earned that name, why it seemed so big at certain times of the year, and so on. Finding facts on the internet wiled away some time and before long I had emailed an impressive amount of information to Barry. Just for good measure, after seeing an intriguing article about a NASA spacecraft currently orbiting the planet Saturn, I sent that as well. It would soon capture pictures of our planet from millions of miles away.

Barry was suitably impressed when he got around to reading the material, piquing his interest to the extent of deciding to post it on his website. We discussed related matters, sharing our insights. It was lovely to see him so enthused.

A different type of grounding took place later, when we popped out to purchase some naturopathic essence to experiment on treating his eczema. He seemed to enjoy strolling around the familiar township, returning books to the library as we went and even donating a few books in good condition that he no longer required. Coincidentally, he was pleased to purchase a couple of bandanas to protect his neck from the sun. Not much as a fashion choice, but certainly provoking some humour as we rummaged through an eclectic bunch of colourfully patterned options.

My wanton eyes were inadvertently drawn to sweet treats as we passed the Mullum Chocolate Shop. I averted my gaze quickly, but not quickly enough to divert him from the tempting assortment. Within moments he was canvasing all the sweet options on offer. Seeking his special flavours took a while as he chatted to Sharon, the friendly owner, behind a high, well-stacked glass counter. Every conceivable sweet treat tempted him. Coloured wrappers, foil wrappers, cellophane tubes, musk sticks, sugar-dusted coatings, soft chewy toffees, bright shiny swirls, barbershop canes, mouth-popping balls, speckled chocolates, liquorice twists, humbugs, marshmallows and jellies. There was so much choice, so many assorted flavours, all reminiscent of childhood. Dipping into almost-forgotten favourites probably promised a sense of comfort in his vulnerable condition. 'Jelly babies,' he said eventually, 'must have jelly babies.' He bought a minimal quantity but they lasted longer than anticipated as his face suddenly contorted with pain from chewing on one. It seems they were definitely *not* a good idea just then.

With so much consideration given to food all his life, Cancerian Barry had been severely out of his element with radiation-affected taste buds. Nothing tasted as he remembered it should. His mouth ulcers caused him a lot of pain. Chewing slowly, he tried (unsuccessfully) to avoid placing food on the ulcerations. He absolutely refused to eat 'mush' or mashed anything. Juices were a maybe. Lack of saliva due to his salivary glands being affected by the radiotherapy added to the problem. Although chewing gum can sometimes appear uncouth, he found it was the only way to get the juices flowing again (one of his doctors had recommended that he try it). He continued with that until the end of the year when dry mouth syndrome ceased to plague him.

He needed to drink plenty of water. Talking his way through even a moderate length conversation or interview made his mouth dry. Prior to cancer, he hadn't been in the habit of keeping water within reach. Now he developed a new routine of keeping a glass of water handy. Unfortunately, he'd accidentally knocked it over his desk with a sweeping hand gesture a couple of times. Cleaning up the spillage irked him — sodden interview notes and books did not please him at all — and he learned the practicalities of keeping the glass out of harm's way pretty quickly.

Barry had been advised to maintain his weight, but he was eating half-quantity meals — and was happy to have lost over seven kilos, weighing below a hundred kilos for the first time in many years. The hospital dietician recommended nutritious food, but he had difficulty swallowing many foodstuffs, even healthy ones. It was a challenge to prepare satisfying meals for him. Stewed apples and pears, dressed up as apple snow — something his mother used to make — was a surprise treat I made one day. His response was very encouraging.

There followed further forays into the kitchen with various outcomes, mostly positive. I lost count of the number of banana bread recipes I tried. Despite a variety of ingredient combinations, they were mostly consumed hungrily. My sensitivity to what he found tolerable seemed to sharpen, with little else to distract me.

I still felt lonesome at times and very distant from my family and friends, feeling I was losing track of their day-to-day events and milestones. Despite the wonders of technology, occasional phone calls and emails had to suffice, but were just not the same as a warm smile, hugging embrace or empathetic cuddle.

19

Emotional Awareness

A fine warm day, shortly after the last treatment, prompted an energetic start to our household chores. A light breeze indicated a good day to catch up on the laundry backlog. Once the line was full, we turned our attention to enjoying a coffee on the deck gazing towards nearby Mount Chincogan. We questioned whether any pressing matters needed resolving. Nothing emerged, and we quietly wandered into meaningful matters of where Barry was at in himself.

He mentioned the inner changes he was experiencing, changes of attitude and valuable lessons learned from the whole process of dealing with cancer. In particular, he identified his previously precipitate behaviour. For example, he had been very prone to road rage and had sometimes reacted foolishly when other drivers had 'done the wrong thing'. Now, instead of bellowing needlessly, he'd become less volatile and, although he still passed judgement on unpredictable and thoughtless drivers, it had become more of a grumble, though not so humble. I was always bemused by his outbursts, as there was no point to them when the other driver couldn't hear him — and what a waste of his own energy to vent like that (as well as unsettling his passengers).

We discussed things like responsibility for personal expression and stress and bottled-up emotions. With all his years reading about spiritual matters in different forms, he recognised there was more to spirituality than superficial perusal. There needed to be a solid foundation of faith, a firm reference point of belief. It was not enough to simply retreat to a meditative comfort zone to de-stress. In suffering Barry had found that he started to better understand his inner life. He realised a greater connection between mind, body and spirit. He's written about his body being the vehicle of the soul — and the journey with cancer has illustrated a responsibility to look after and protect it. Being productive in life is about more than earning money for money's sake, and he recognised the need to use his personal skills and resources diligently, with the best intentions for himself and others.

Barry developed greater appreciation of people who worked generously to alleviate suffering. His general demeanour softened. He became more tolerant of others' foibles, and was able to shed some of his misconceptions about personality traits that he'd found disagreeable in the past.

It seemed to be enough to tentatively air these things about the crisis in his life even briefly, to acknowledge that we were both in a process of change. Living with cancer prior to the diagnosis, changes had already been happening in his body without his knowledge. At first, wanting to heal the cancer itself had been the main objective. Since then, he's been gradually realising that growing through this extreme experience will subtly bring about other changes, with a different form of healing.

20

Birthday

My daughter Tanya arrived to stay for a few days. It was wonderful to see her. It was just before Barry's birthday and he wanted to show her around the area, to visit places that were special to him. He perked up remarkably when we went to picturesque Broken Head, south of Byron Bay. He enjoyed pointing out significant landmarks along the scenic shoreline and was especially thrilled to see a dolphin surfing the breakers. Eagerly we looked and waited for more, but none appeared. A lone dolphin sending us a message?

In Greek mythology, dolphins were reputed to guide ships through turbulent waters and to rescue seafarers in hazardous situations. There are many stories throughout time of dolphins bonding with humans, and there are numerous accounts of them rescuing people in danger. It's been said that they are known as the only creature who loves humans for their own sake. I like to think that seeing the dolphin that day was a reassuring and uplifting symbol of rescue and recovery.

We walked along a winding clifftop path with overhanging native trees providing shade and obscuring the sky. Emerging onto an open grassy space, we looked down to see three young boys with fishing lines descend the sheer cliff face to a ledge below. Wind-tousled hair and flapping jackets, they were oblivious to their audience, as we watched in trepidation at their daring. Seeing them arrive safely at their ledge, we caught our breath and continued.

Tanya must have been inspired, as she then went ahead, skirting a tiny sandy cove to climb up a rocky cliff face opposite. She was quite adroit and found plenty of hand and foot holds. I was taken by surprise to see how high she ventured with relative ease. My mothering instincts already activated by the antics of the three boys was being tested further. Apparently climbing was Tanya's recently learned hobby and she was testing her skills. I was relieved when she returned safely and joined Barry to continue walking and chatting amicably while I took photos.

Later, after Tanya's departure, Barry's daughter and granddaughter Isabella invited us to join them for his birthday lunch at Liliana's Café in the beautifully renovated 101-year-old Possum Creek Schoolhouse. Set in a picturesque rainforest environment, featuring original artefacts and with scrumptious cuisine, we're glad to have shared that experience with them. It had only opened in 2012 and unfortunately has now closed.

Although food would normally play an important part in any birthday celebration for Barry, his seventy-first birthday could have ended up being quite tame. He and I did make a special point of going to a regional cinema to enjoy the annual screening from Europe of Andre Rieu's fabulous concert at Maastricht. Andre's showmanship, the rousing music and colourful costumes were a delight and we happily swayed and clapped in appreciation.

However, the real highlight was Wimbledon. Barry's interest in tennis goes back a long way, so the Wimbledon men's singles title was top priority, no matter what time of night it was televised. Watching the Scottish player Andy Murray trade some unbelievable shots with Novak Djokovic and win some awesome points was truly inspirational. Barry was brimming with emotion watching the tough finish and elated to have seen the record-breaking win for Andy Murray.

It was a thrilling way to mark his birthday after all.

Some months later, I saw an article in the *Fiji Times* of 2 February 2014, which clarified some of Barry's Chinese astrological background for 2014, another Year of the Horse. The horse represented travel, competition and victory and it was a symbol of nobility, freedom and leadership. People born under that sign are intuitive and have keen judgement. Oprah Winfrey, Jackie Chan, Denzel Washington and John Travolta were among the people born in horse years, who are characterised by being cheerful, bright, popular and fun-loving and like crowds, people and parties. Barry's quite pleased to be in the company of that select group of celebrities born in the Year of the Horse and he's certainly had a keen interest in current affairs and anything to do with the entertainment industry — and from all accounts has attended more than his fair share of parties.

In later years though, he has found he can't tolerate congested locations and over-crowded roadways. He's still keen on travel and is always on the look-out for the next holiday destination. His intuition is usually spot-on.

21

Behind the Façade

It was time to face the next phase — my return home — which was a new start emotionally for both of us. I faced a comprehensive clearing of accumulated possessions. Somehow it took two hours to trawl through so it would all fit in my luggage. We shared a breakfast on the deck in the warm winter sun, with the distant mountain bestowing a silent blessing towards us. Miscellaneous birds serenaded around us. It was so tempting to 'linga longa' and let time take its own course. Time fracture and time warps had been recently discussed and now we were embarking on another split segment of the path.

We chatted quietly on the trip to Gold Coast airport. So much had happened since my arrival in Brisbane seven weeks earlier. This time, though, the worry about unknown medical procedures was behind us. Barry's first medical check-up was still ahead, but he was not fussed about it because he was feeling so much better. I embraced his confidence and felt our closeness would survive whatever happened.

Pulling into the airport departure terminal seemed an anticlimax. Barry pulled my suitcase from the car boot and

I gathered my hand luggage. We faced each other and he thanked me again for being with him throughout his ordeal. Our farewell looked like it was going to be fairly ordinary, a peck on the cheek and off I'd go. But no, simultaneously we reached out to each other and embraced warmly. Hugs mean a lot to me — and this one spoke volumes. I recognised a genuine positive connectedness. Barriers were down between us. We could look directly at each other without a veil of superficial gestures. Our masks were briefly put aside. We could finally share our very real love for each other.

As I recall our loving farewell, I'm reminded of an article I read in the waiting room at the hospital. It had such an impact that I had copied it as a reminder to revisit the feelings it stirred in me. It was by bestselling author Dr Martha Beck, who is 'one of the smartest women I know,' according to Oprah Winfrey. Beck said, 'To care for someone can mean to adore them, feed them, tend their wounds. But *care* can also signify sorrow, as in "bowed down by cares" or investment in an outcome, such as "who cares?" The word *love* has no such range of meaning: it's pure acceptance.' She continued, 'Real healing, real love comes from people who are both totally committed to helping — and able to emotionally detach.'

Beck also said, 'I really do think that any deep crisis is an opportunity to make your life extraordinary in some way.'

I had done some soul-searching before I read this article. I'd been harbouring some resentment about not pursuing my own aims and objectives. During a discussion with a friend of mine around that time, we'd mentioned 'putting my life on hold', which reflected my feeling of being unfulfilled. Was that really the case? Different areas of interest had emerged while I'd been with Barry on that visit, one being this writing — he'd asked me to record my observations. Another of my long-term interests was photography, which had always been encouraged by my father and now by Barry. I had also done some culinary experiments too, which were enjoyable. Was my whole experience about finding some authenticity buried in the void of myself?

I recently saw an advertising slogan, 'the destination of *quality* luggage', and my mind saw the word 'baggage'. I found myself wondering where do we take our personal emotional baggage? What is the destination or goal that we take it to? It must be *quality* or we wouldn't be carrying the burden of it — would we? After consideration, maybe I could continue where I'm going in life, towards my ultimate destination, without too much of it.

There had been very real moments during those past weeks when I'd felt as if new growth was tentatively sprouting from within. The fragility of it expressed vulnerability. It needed to be nurtured and encouraged to flourish. At the same time, something in me stole the right to do so, leaving me feeling the void, not accepting or deserving this opportunity. Well, that is also part of me, so, recalling a family adage that *we Hills women have had to learn to be strong*, I'll grab my watering can and gently nudge that sprout to fruitfulness.

Realistically, I'm now in touch with my creative spark (sprout). So here I am writing. And, yes, it was due to Barry asking me to make a note of how things impacted me, as we trod this unfamiliar path.

His vulnerability had become more evident the deeper he was captured by the radiotherapy. Somehow a different identity was being revealed after more than fifty years of professional cover-up. In the past, we had discussed the way we all wear our 'personality' masks. We laughed at times when I mentioned a kind of transfiguration taking place — because

I had seen a quick shadow of a different side of him, or different face, to the one he normally revealed. So now, as he was unable to sustain so much of the façade, I saw perhaps for the first time what I'd only sensed before. He had previously acted out the character of fitting me into a 'suitable' role in line with his status. He'd been rather autocratic and didn't always appreciate my opinion or what was important to me. With his changing demeanour, understanding, compassion and acceptance were emerging.

Without the falseness, I could genuinely respond to the care and attention he needed with the detachment required to see things objectively and without the subconscious role playing. There was a very real possibility of harmonising and balancing our two different personas. Cautiously, my defences were lowering. Detachment can be a wonderful measure of objectivity. Love — let's make it without judgement or criticism or bitterness. Let's try peace and calm and caring. Indulge in laughter, wonderment and delight. Dispense with anxiety and stress. Give relaxation a go. Omit anger and control. Accept without the need to change.

I experienced feelings of unreality on the plane home. Efforts to distract myself with Sudoku were unsuccessful — I made a mistake and was not able to back-track to correct it. Have a drink, close my eyes. A brief respite.

Arriving home, my main concern was chatting to Barry's son Matt on the phone for a 'debrief' session. He would be staying with Barry for a short time. The call was meant to be a quick overview conveying necessary information to help get the best value from their companionable time together. My tea was cold by the time I returned to it.

The overview chiefly noted Barry's eczema being the outstanding problem. The mouth ulcers were less painful and his dental program was in place. The burned skin around his neck and shoulders had softened and was not causing too much discomfort, although he still needed to wear a cravat or scarf when outside and a hat when in the sun. His weight had steadied. His diet was improving. His heart hadn't shown any cause for concern lately. My main concern was his thyroid function since he had forgotten his morning Thyroxin tablets recently and become very tired driving home on the expressway after taking Tanya to the airport. I'd seen his tiredness then and offered to drive, but he was unable to stop on the motorway. His determination to work through it was commendable, but he did collapse for a sleep on reaching home. That degree of tiredness was an indicator of reduced thyroid function and could have resulted in an accident. It was something to watch out for and to take into account when planning activities.

Back in my local environment, I was heartened to be greeted by a number of people who asked after Barry. They were all moved to hear of his experiences, and some expressed admiration at his level of faith which had brought him through relatively unscathed, or at least which had given him the strength to endure so much. His reaction was humbling when I told him how people were so concerned for his wellbeing. Some had been praying and sending healing thoughts to him and were delighted to know he had fared so well.

I felt gratitude that there were so many considerate people in my neighbourhood — their phone calls, smiles and hugs were all so very welcoming. I feel so fortunate to be in their midst.

Smartly back into the habit of an evening walk with my gorgeous dog, just over a week after my return I suddenly remembered something I needed to tell Barry. I called his mobile and brought him up to date. Before long he's telling me that, as a result of my call, he's been inspired to take a walk as we're talking and was half way down the street already! It had been almost impossible to persuade him to take a walk, even though it had been recommended for health reasons. He chuckled as he shared this surprise, triggering my laughter in response. So beautifully simple, mischievous and a real togetherness, despite 800 kilometres distance between us.

A few hours later, as I sat quietly cosy and content on the carpet in the light of my glowing log fire with white fluffy dog happily alongside, I was jolted by the phone ringing. It was a friend from the UK calling to tell of a bizarre accident that had happened to her the previous week. In the course of taking her dog for an evening stroll to a park across the road from where she lived, she was walloped on the back of her head with a football and knocked sprawling to the ground. It took four strong men to carry her back across the road and up to her apartment. After medical consultations, she was found to have fractures and bruising, requiring various aids to assist her movement and needed ongoing care to help with personal grooming. She was phoning to ask if Barry and I could mobilise our prayers and healing and send it her way. With all the help that Barry had received, how perfect to be able to reciprocate.

22

Four Weeks After the End of Treatment

A call from Barry who was very upset because he'd lost his Visa card. He'd looked everywhere, retraced his steps, called places he'd visited — no sign of it. He reiterated some of his observations about his state of health recently. The previous Wednesday he'd been 'woolly headed' at tennis, and then at Saturday tennis again – still saying he was woolly headed – he'd played one set okay but the second one was not so good. But hey, he did play two sets. He had been concerned at having mislaid not only his Visa card now, but his Mastercard a few weeks earlier. He had reluctantly re-set passwords. The tediousness of remembering a number of different passwords — he was not willing to write them down for security reasons — was perturbing. Rhyming and word play seemed to help a bit but he felt discombobulated. He can still be stubborn and intent on doing things his own way. Some things haven't changed.

One thing evident in all that was how subdued he was about the loss — there were none of his usual high-velocity outbursts.

As he progressed back to 'normality', albeit with a 'woolly' head, it seemed to take more effort and concentration to achieve what previously would have been very ordinary and simple feats. Being a little absentminded was at times bothersome, especially when he fell back into platitudes like 'it happens to everyone' or 'everyone does that'. Since he'd always had a very good memory, as well as a good measure of awareness of amounts and quantities, it was disconcerting to find him becoming forgetful and trying to cover up irregularities. Processing mental tasks and remembering times and dates had to be converted to writing notes. Some would say that at his age, short-term memory loss was a feature many experienced, and not just due to cancer treatment. However, the problem seemed to have developed at the time of his treatment and there were some abilities he had previously taken for granted that were more affected.

The Cancer.Net site refers to symptoms of difficulty thinking clearly as 'chemo brain', even for those not having chemotherapy. Apparently it's particularly relevant with radiation treatment to the head and neck. With all those weeks of radiation directed to that region, is it any wonder Barry was a little woolly headed. We just needed to keep tabs on some of the fine detail to help him through, and value whatever was obviously going well whenever possible.

Several days passed, and no sign of his lost credit card. Then, unexpectedly, it was found. Very simply, no drama, it turned up and everything was on track for him again.

23

Three-month Check-up

Neeeding to renew his doctor's referral letter, Barry made an appointment to see his local general practitioner. While there, he was asked to bare himself to scrutiny once more, to check his skin condition.

He was unusually quiet when he phoned me later that day. None of his usual buoyancy, which had sustained him throughout the long year's events, was evident. No jocular comments, only a barely audible, 'Guess what?'

My response was hesitant. I didn't want to *guess* anything about this doctor's visit, which was expected to be nothing more than ordinary but which now seemed to be anything but ordinary. His gruff voice announced, 'Five potentially troublesome spots were found. I have to have biopsies.'

What? Hasn't he been through enough turmoil already? I was incredulous that there may be more to come. Surgeons wielding scalpels were haunting us. This can't be happening, surely.

Obviously he had to undergo the biopsies, and with heartfelt relief we were glad to see that the results showed the spots were benign. He looked a little strange when I saw him, with little white dressing spots covering the wounds, but his huge smile restored his appearance. He was so glad to have something so significant to smile about.

24

Short Break

With so much unusual and unexpected activity during the year, it was time to get away from it all and take off on a short break. We would cross the continent and head for Perth for a week's rest and recreation. There was a lot to recover from.

I had booked a holiday resort near the beautiful Margaret River region, on the southwest coast. It was advertised as an eco-lodge resort and seemed just the place for a calm relaxing holiday.

We flew into Perth late afternoon, collected our hire car and drove south into the dusky evening through unexpected rain. It was dark when we arrived two hours later and drove down a sparse bush track. We collected our key from a mail box and wondered what we were getting ourselves into when we entered the lodge we'd booked. Ten minutes was all it took to see what a mistake we'd made. Some creative photography had given a completely false impression of the accommodation. It was scruffy and dirty and far from the condition and standard we expected — and certainly did no justice to the title of resort. Tired after the long trip from Sydney, Barry's grumblings began to escalate.

Within twenty minutes I was on the internet searching for alternative accommodation in the region. Unfortunately we could not find anywhere else for that night. Sleep on it and something will show up tomorrow. We hardly wanted to touch anything, let alone sleep in stained bedding. We reluctantly managed to sort out something halfway acceptable.

First thing in the morning I was on the laptop again, and within minutes found a B&B almost an hour's drive away. And they had a vacancy!

We couldn't exit the lodge quickly enough. However, I did need to hand back the keys and the feedback form which Barry had completed (which obviously was not at all complimentary). He stayed in the car while I did that, not trusting himself to keep a civil tongue. When faced with our hasty retreat, we were offered another lodge. But Barry was in no mood to be placated and anyway, he reasoned, why couldn't they have given us a lodge that was in better condition in the first place. We sped off, car wheels spinning on the gravel to emphasise our need to be out of there as quickly as possible.

We arrived at the charming Yalgorup Country Lodge to be met by the owner Janet, who warmly welcomed us to her best room, which had high ceilings and was elegantly decorated with comfortable furniture. Even the cat was amicable. We could feel the healing effects of the homely atmosphere and delightful gardens almost immediately. With a restful recreation area, library nook and charming country dining area, we began to relax and feel at ease.

Once ensconced in our suite, we enjoyed a refreshing brew, orientated ourselves with help from our informative hostess and happily embarked on a casual walk to check out our surrounds. What a delight to discover a picturesque waterway just around the corner. Nature's quiet brought solace. We lingered, took photos and absorbed the restful ambience. It was just what we needed.

During the following days, we were delighted to meet up with long-time friends and enjoyed wandering around, chatting and exploring the region with them. Dianne and her husband Roy have travelled their own very long and remarkable journey through the debilitating symptoms of multiple sclerosis.

We reluctantly farewelled them and our hosts in Yalgorup and made our way north to Fremantle to meet up with friends and relatives there. We did indulge in a little 'grand' accommodation at the Esplanade Hotel and loved the lively waterfront area and its unique characteristics — an excellent choice for socialising as well as for delectable seafood. We felt very spoilt and decided that, despite a poor start to our trip, we had ended up with it being so much better than anticipated. The recuperative effects of delightful accommodation, warm friendships, embracing relatives and the amazing ambience of Western Australian congeniality had proved to be the best choice we could have made at the time.

We returned to Sydney feeling invigorated and ready to face almost anything with renewed enthusiasm.

25

Postscript

A year later I was back up north, and a specialist diagnosed that Barry's most recent bout of skin irritation was the result of a yeast infection and an overabundance of sugar in his system. He believed the diagnosis, on his seventy-second birthday, was literally an answer to his prayers. It was something he could work with, something he could physically tackle. Eliminating all forms of sugar from his diet for a few weeks? No problem! Nothing was going to deter him. He became fixated on eliminating all sugars, including fructose.

Alcohol, with its sugar content, was definitely off limits for the duration as well, although not for long if he could help it. But each time he tried a sip, he was disappointed that it hadn't improved in flavour. It wasn't until well over twelve months after the end of treatment that he could appreciate an occasional glass of good quality red wine with dinner.

The pain of his flesh had been unbearable at times, resulting in distress so fierce that it was hard to determine cause and effect in the continuous cycle of skin eruption and stress response. He couldn't stop scratching his reddened irritated skin, which triggered a bacterial infection and obviously worsened his condition. That set in motion the sugar detox initiative.

After two months on the sugar-free regime, when he began to re-introduce fruit and certain vegetables to his diet he was careful not to overdo it. And definitely there was no indulging in ice cream. He did take to coconut yoghurt though, which is a delicious and much healthier alternative he tells me.

His skin only started to fade from fire-engine redness after two months of restraint, but was not cured. Over time he's tried innumerable lotions and potions in his endeavours to stop the irritation. With the heat of summer, and wanting to continue playing tennis without getting sunburned, he purchased a lightweight long-sleeved tennis shirt which proved to be indispensable.

His doctor and health advisors worked cooperatively over many months, which led to many other significant changes in diet, a significant improvement in his skin condition, as well as an improvement in his health and general demeanour.

As I was writing about this, my heart expanded at the sound of the warm, honeyed tones of a song precious to us both, 'Somewhere Over the Rainbow', faintly wafting over the airwaves. For me, the song is a poignant reminder of rising above our troubles and seeing the beauty and colours of a wonderful world.

PART III
Matt's Story

by Matt Eaton

Being an astrologer born under the sign of Cancer, I'm sure it must have occurred to my father in darker moments that one day that word might come back to bite him.

Like many people in the 1970s, he had been a serious sun-worshipper at one point. I remember him using Hawaiian Tropic to baste himself for the baking. I remember the tans and the nude beach on Sydney Harbour he frequented for some time after he and my mother divorced. I guess we all thought this would be where the price might eventually be paid in the Big C stakes. As it turned out, someone else close to us would be forced to follow that path. Baz was to walk a different road.

As I remember it, Dad told me he had cancer just days after we learned my stepfather Dave Lindsay was suffering from secondary cancer resulting from an undetected melanoma. Mum had been married to Dave for a quarter of a century and he had become a second father to me. We knew from the moment it was detected that his cancer was a death sentence. For us to discover at virtually the same time that Barry was also dealing with cancer left our family reeling at the cruel game that fate had decided to play upon us.

From the outset, as everyone does, we determined to face it all with a default mindset of positivity. This state of mind was to become a critical factor in Barry's approach to the next twelve months. No doubt it helps when doctors tell you your cancer is operable and your chances of complete recovery are very good. Dad and I knew all too well that Dave was not going to be so lucky and I think that's one of the reasons he dug so deep in facing up to the situation.

However, when Baz found out he had not one but two types of cancer in his body, I imagine it must have felt like two brick walls collapsing on him at once.

It all started with a lump in his throat that was making it difficult for him to swallow. From this, following several examinations and tests, we eventually learned he had two cancers, seemingly unrelated, in the thyroid and the tongue. Unrelated, except that both of them could potentially affect his voice, the part of Barry that lay at the core of his identity as a radio presenter and voiceover artist.

I clearly remember the times, aged eight or nine, I would follow him to work in Sydney to watch him put a weekend radio program to air on Sunday afternoons on the ABC. Those experiences of being let loose in the ABC record library and wandering through the studios in the old Forbes Street complex, or being allowed to stand behind the cameras on Saturday afternoons when he hosted *Sportsview* on ABC TV, helped inform my decision later to pursue radio reporting and producing. Those times are imprinted upon my childhood memory.

The prognosis for his long-term health was good, but having to deal with the risk of losing the quality of the voice upon which he had based his living for so long seemed like a rather cruel irony. Hard to swallow.

Removing his thyroid — which is so close to the vocal chords — was just the first step in many months of treatment. The surgery occurred at John Flynn Hospital at Tugun on the Gold Coast, which was relatively close to Barry's home in northern New South Wales.

It all went without a hitch. The procedure went well —
there were no complications and no negative impacts on the
voice. He would, of course, need to take thyroid hormone
replacement pills for the rest of his life. But that was a small
price to pay. Baz accepted this with good grace, although I
knew full well how much this tablet dependency galled him.
Neither he nor his partner Anne are great fans of modern
medicine and its reliance on pharmaceuticals and surgery. But
what choice did he have?

To be honest, my immediate and ongoing concern had been
that the two of them would compare notes and Baz would dig
his heels in and refuse medical interventions from here on.
The thing was, I knew only too well there was no such thing
as an effective alternative treatment for cancer. It was clear
to me that any attempt in this regard was, in the words of
Alistair MacLean, the way to dusty death.

To get through this it was going to be a matter of following
doctors' orders.

Round two promised to be a lot tougher on that front. My
late stepfather Dave, a thoracic physician and a very good
diagnostician, had told me flat out that the only effective
treatment for cancer of the tongue would be six to seven
weeks of radiotherapy.

Radiation.

From the conversations we'd had thus far, Barry was not
at all predisposed towards going down this path. He had
already told me that, no matter what, he would never agree to
chemotherapy. Lucky for him, I discovered this wouldn't be
necessary. Nevertheless, I started to prepare myself for a fight.

Though Dad lives in northern New South Wales, it was
made clear to us the best place to seek help was Royal Brisbane

Hospital, which runs one of the largest cancer treatment services in the country. We were assured this was where the very best medical opinions would be on offer.

At this point we assumed that he'd be able to return to John Flynn Hospital for the second round of his treatment, although I'm not certain whether Dad was clear about what that treatment would entail.

Once a month, Royal Brisbane Hospital runs a cancer roundtable in which new patients are poked and prodded by a parade of the hospital's cancer specialists. Those doctors then go away and collectively decide upon the best method of treatment for each person.

Dad asked me to accompany him the day he attended the cancer clinic, saying he wasn't sure how much of it he would be able to take in and that I might need to take notes. It was obvious by this time that he was having a tough time trying to cope with it all.

I went into reporter mode. The cancer centre at the hospital runs like a well-oiled machine. We were whisked into a treatment room where oncologists, surgeons and haematologists paraded in and out, examining, asking questions and making notes.

It very quickly became clear, as I knew it would, that the only treatment on offer would be radiotherapy. Baz accepted the news with good grace, but I could see he was at the outer limits in his efforts to keep it together. I scribbled notes and asked questions when he forgot to do so.

Specialists arrived and left and we had a chance to talk in between their visits.

At one point a nurse who had remained in the room after the doctors departed began assuring us the radiotherapy treatment facility in Brisbane was excellent. 'No, no,' Barry told her, 'I want to get my treatment at John Flynn Hospital.'

The nurse looked at us in utter bewilderment. It finally dawned on her that something important hadn't been made clear to us. She knuckled down and explained that Brisbane was one of only a handful of hospitals in Australia with its own tomotherapy machine — and that Barry was incredibly lucky to have this treatment available to him. It delivered radiotherapy in a much more focused way, targeting just the cancerous tissue and reducing the severity of long-term side-effects. Brisbane obtained a tomotherapy machine in 2011, the first hospital in Australia to do so. John Flynn Hospital, excellent though it is, has no tomotherapy facility.

With the clinic ended, we had an hour or so to get a coffee while we awaited the outcome of the doctors' roundtable discussion. Now Baz had something new to swallow. He would need to receive radiotherapy *and* he would have to do it in Brisbane, which was two hours' drive away from the comforts of home.

I was pleased and proud of the way he responded to it all, because he could see now that he had to do it their way.

It became obvious he would need to relocate to Brisbane for the duration of his treatment, as so many other cancer patients had done before him. This was a bit of a shock to the system but it was really a no-brainer to agree to the tomotherapy treatment given its clear advantages.

The side-effects of radiotherapy vary in severity from person to person. But we were told it was impossible to avoid some level of permanent impact. First, there was the burning from the treatment itself. This was temporary, but would become quite painful towards the end of the treatment. The radiation would also start to make him feel very unwell, which was another reason he would need to be staying close by.

As unpleasant a prospect as all of that must have been, to my mind the long-term impacts were the scariest thing facing him — how the radiation would impact on saliva glands, for instance. We were told to expect permanent reduction in saliva production and there was an outside chance he could suffer total saliva shutdown, although the oncologist now in charge of Barry's case, Dr Charles Lin, was confident he would be able to avoid this outcome. There was also likely to be a permanent impact on his taste buds — some foods would forever taste different, and spicy foods might become totally unpalatable.

The up side was that Dr Lin gave him a 95 per cent chance of complete recovery. No more cancer.

Before the radiotherapy began, the next step in the process was to consult a dentist at the Brisbane Dental Hospital. He read Barry the riot act, explaining that because his saliva production would be compromised his teeth would face a much greater risk of serious decay without a new regimen of fluoride treatment that he would need to adopt from this day forward, for richer or poorer. The dentist proceeded to show us terrifying pictures of mouths in which teeth had rotted to stumps because said treatment had been ignored. He assured us this was the inevitable result if Barry didn't follow the dentist's instructions precisely twice a day. Jaw necrosis looked somewhat worse than leprosy. I don't know about Dad, but this guy scared the crap out of me.

Weeks later, well into his radiotherapy treatment and faring remarkably well, Dad told me he'd received a phone call from an old friend named Garry Wiseman. This was a man who had trained him in the arts of astrology. Garry told Dad he was really pleased that he had agreed to radiotherapy

— that it was the only way to treat cancer if you wanted to actually stay alive because alternative treatments didn't work. He pointed out that if alternative cancer treatments hadn't been able to save the life of Apple co-founder Steve Jobs, what hope did the rest of us have?

This bolstered Dad's resolve, particularly as he saw Garry as someone who, like him, was not automatically predisposed towards conventional approaches to healing.

Dad did, though, keep one card up his sleeve in this regard and it proved to be enormously beneficial. He had access to something called a crystal bed, used in combination with meditation to augment natural healing. If the crystal bed did nothing more than place him in a regular meditative state and boost his positive approach to the treatment, that alone made it worth its weight in gold. Dad firmly maintains it did much more than that, and I am perfectly willing to accept this at face value. I honestly don't know if it would work for anyone less open-minded.

The most impressive thing for me in the whole experience of Dad's cancer treatment is the way he maintained his positive mental attitude. This, teamed with regular trips home for sessions on his crystal bed, got him through the treatment and out the other side in remarkably good shape.

He told me Dr Lin couldn't believe he had made it through the entire course of treatment without strong painkillers. Dad said he simply didn't need them.

After seven weeks of radiation, his upper chest was burned and his throat was raw, but he wasn't a sickly hulk huddled on the couch. He still had an appetite and was living a fairly normal life, thanks in great part to the support of Anne, who was there for him in those last few weeks of treatment.

There were certainly long-term impacts on his salivary glands and taste buds, but I would describe those side-effects as mild to moderate. But for Baz, the end result was nothing short of remarkable.

Afterword

by Barry Eaton

The search for the magical answer to cure cancer would seem to still be a long way off, but we all live in hope and optimism.

The news of rock legend David Bowie's passing in 2016 shocked the world. Coming just a few days after the release of his much awaited new album *Blackstar*, it was completely unexpected by those outside his inner circle. Bowie had kept his battle with liver cancer a secret for eighteen months, before finally succumbing.

In 2011 Steve Jobs, the founder of Apple, passed from complications following the diagnosis of pancreatic cancer in 2003. Jobs allegedly expressed regret at only using alternative treatments for his cancer — he had chosen not to go down the route of mainstream treatments of chemotherapy and radiation. However, he is reported to have had a liver transplant from a metastasis two years before he passed and took immune suppressing anti-rejection drugs. Mainstream doctors later confirmed that complications from this operation may have caused his death.

Cancer Council Australia states that, 'the five year survival rate for people diagnosed with pancreatic cancer is around

7%'. Yet Steve Jobs survived for some eight years *only* using alternative treatments. Would he have extended his life even further by combining mainstream treatments with his alternative practices? We will never know.

Can we just dismiss complementary medicines and treatment out of hand simply because certain medical authorities are closed-minded sceptics and reject anything outside of the mainstream pharmaceutical arena? I believe it becomes a matter for each patient to make these decisions, one way or another after doing careful research.

More and more people are questioning the mainstream methods of chemotherapy and radiotherapy and are looking for less invasive answers to this insidious disease. Such treatment is even coming under question from the establishment. In 2015 the American Cancer Council released a document entitled 'Second Cancers in Adults' which raised the question 'How does radiation therapy and chemotherapy affect the risk of second cancers?' I recommend the ACS website for those interested in pursuing this revealing line of investigation (www.cancer.org/acs/groups/cid/documents/webcontent/002043-pdf.pdf).

Ongoing Research

In 2015 Ty and Charlene Bollinger produced *The Truth About Cancer, A Global Quest*, a controversial nine-part documentary video series for 'the courageous person who is seeking to reverse cancer or prevent cancer while seeking a natural approach to healing'. They travelled firstly across the United States and then around the rest of the world interviewing top scientists, doctors, researchers and cancer patients who are 'preventing, treating and beating cancer', according to the transcripts of the interviews.

It is a fascinating compendium of research and information first released on the internet and now available in DVD and book form, and it certainly challenges many mainstream medical beliefs.

However it seems that we may also be on the verge of significant breakthroughs in the mainstream field of cancer research.

A news story released in early 2016 said that US scientists have announced they may have made a cancer treatment breakthrough, by using a patient's own immune cells to treat leukaemia. Professor Stanley Riddell, an immunotherapy researcher at the world renowned Fred Hutchison Cancer Research Centre in Seattle, stated that using treated immune cells wiped out cancer in twenty-seven of twenty-nine patients with acute lymphoblastic leukaemia in one trial. A small but encouraging trial. The patients had previously failed all other treatments. Cancer was also reduced in six out of seven patients whose cancer had spread. Unfortunately there were some serious side effects in the latest trials, including two deaths. So it would appear that while immunotherapy may be a promising line of research, it is still in its very early days of testing.

My ongoing research has certainly made me sit up and think about my own cancer journey and how things are constantly changing. With the number of people of all ages now being diagnosed with this insidious disease, it's heartening to see so much information coming to light.

About the authors

Barry Eaton

Well known in the radio industry, Barry Eaton has wide experience in the media and entertainment industries, with many years with the Australian Broadcasting Corporation and various commercial radio and TV stations. His work includes news and sports anchoring, lifestyle shows, current affairs, talkback radio, starring on ABC TV in a current affairs-style feature film about the Gallipoli landing, and co-hosting *Good Morning Sydney* on Channel 10. He currently hosts and produces RadioOutThere.com, an internet radio show which has a worldwide audience. He is also a voice-over artist, narrating documentary films, radio and TV commercials. He co-hosted the spectacular 2006 ANZAC Military Tattoo at Sydney's Superdome (now Acer Arena) and The Tattoo Spectacular in Perth in 2007.

Barry originally trained as an actor and he returned to the stage in Agatha Christie's play *The Hollow* in Sydney in 2006. He has also appeared in a number of films and TV shows.

As coordinator of the Faculty of Journalism at Macleay College in Sydney from 1995–99, he lectured in radio journalism and production. He also has wide corporate experience, running his own company, which specialised in media consulting, video and audio production and special event marketing and publicity. He now consults to Spokesperson Media Training as a corporate trainer.

Barry studied astrology in 1991 and then embarked an ongoing exploration of the mysteries of life and what lies beyond. Since then he has also developed his abilities as a psychic intuitive and a medium, which led to his first book *Afterlife* (2011), followed by *No Goodbyes* (2013).

He has written articles, newspaper columns and travel features for the *Sun Herald* and *Theatre Australia*, scripted documentary films, commercials and corporate presentations, and co-wrote the screenplay for two feature films with his son Matt.

Anne Morjanoff

Anne Morjanoff had a 15-year career in Sydney's central bank, beginning in communications and moving to the human resources department. As enrolment officer at the parent-run pre-school her daughters attended, she sourced funding to build a new purpose built pre-school on Sydney's northern beaches.

Anne developed a passion for number symbolism, using it to re-assure many people of their life conditions and conducting workshops on the power of numbers in everyday life. Anne travelled with her daughters for many years when they competed in ice-skating competitions, including in European events. She has been a dressmaker for a fashion boutique, and now works in the education arena in a casual administrative role.